Security Implications of SDI

WILL WE BE MORE SECURE IN 2010?

Security Implications of SDI

WILL WE BE MORE SECURE IN 2010?

Edited by Jeffrey Simon
with an Introduction by Fred Charles Iklé

1990

NATIONAL DEFENSE UNIVERSITY PRESS
Fort Lesley J. McNair
Washington, DC 20319-6000

National Defense University Press Publications

To increase general knowledge and inform discussion, NDU Press publishes books on subjects relating to US national security.

Each year, in this effort, the National Defense University, through the Institute for National Strategic Studies, hosts about two dozen Senior Fellows who engage in original research on national security issues. NDU Press publishes the best of this research.

In addition, the Press publishes other especially timely or distinguished writing on national security, as well as new editions of out-of-print defense classics, and books based on University-sponsored conferences concerning national security affairs.

NDU Press publications are sold by the US Government Printing Office. For ordering information, call (202) 783-3238 or write to the Superintendent of Documents, US Government Printing Office, Washington, DC 20402

Library of Congress Cataloging in Publication Data
Security implications of SDI : will we be more secure in 2010? / edited by Jeffrey Simon.
    p.   cm. #20759443
    "Evolved from a conference held in April 1986 sponsored by the Mobilization Concepts Development Center, Institute for National Strategic Studies, National Defense University; the Strategic Studies Institute of the US Army War College; and the American Enterprise Institute"—Pref.
    Includes bibliographical references.
    $10.00 (est.)
    1. Strategic Defense Initiative. 2. Soviet Union—Defenses. I. Simon, Jeffrey. 1942-   . II. National Defense University. Mobilization Concepts Development Center. III. Army War College (U.S.). Strategic Studies Institute. IV. American Enterprise Institute for Public Policy Research.
UG743.S43   1989
358.1'754—dc20
                        89-13947
                        CIP

First printing, March 1990

CONTENTS

ILLUSTRATIONS

FOREWORD

The current debate as to whether the Strategic Defense Initiative will make this nation more secure by the year 2010 rests on the question of whether such weapons might be developed and deployed by that time. The question is a complex one, involving political commitment, economic strength, and technological accomplishment, as well as international conditions. But if SDI is assumed to play even a minor role in US national strategy, then the needs of that strategy for the next century must be anticipated now.

Toward that goal, Dr. Jeffrey Simon has assembled in this anthology the views of specialists on the issue. What they see varies, not surprisingly, according to assumptions and forecasts in such areas as technological feasibility and the progress of arms control. They agree that SDI would have inescapable consequences for our force structure and relations with our allies and adversaries. They offer valuable insights from their particular areas of expertise. And, in the final section, three of them reach persuasive—yet distinctly different—conclusions about SDI and the long-range security of the United States.

Although the world is far removed from an ideal one made perfectly safe against the threat of offensive nuclear arms, the issue of strategic defense as a complement to offensive arms will continue to attract interest and stir controversy. The range of that interest—and controversy—is thoroughly explored in this book.

J. A. BALDWIN
Vice Admiral, US Navy
President, National Defense
University

ACKNOWLEDGMENTS

This book evolved from a conference held in 1986 sponsored by the Mobilization Concepts Development Center, Institute for National Strategic Studies, National Defense University; the Strategic Studies Institute of the US Army War College; and the American Enterprise Institute. The conference participants, drawn from the academic world and government, came together to discuss the security implications of the Strategic Defense Initiative.

Eleven specialists discuss in this book potential long-term implications of SDI on US security; its impact on US doctrine and force structure, on relations with the USSR, and with the NATO alliance. Finally, three experts, addressing the question "Will We Be More Secure in 2010?" present a divergence of opinion.

I want to express my appreciation to Lieutenant General Richard D. Lawrence, who was President of the National Defense University when this conference was convened; to Lieutenant General Bradley C. Hosmer, who succeeded General Lawrence as President of NDU; to Dr. John E. Endicott, Director, Institute for National Strategic Studies; and to William B. Taylor, Jr., Director, Mobilization Concepts Development Center, for their support during the conference. In addition, I would like to thank Robert J. Pranger and Roger Labrie, formerly of the American Enterprise Institute, and Lieutenant General James E. Thompson, former Commandant of the US Army War College and Lieutenant Colonel Douglas V. Johnson II of the Strategic Studies Institute for their enormous assistance in planning as well as during the conference. I would also like to acknowledge the participation at the conference of Dr. Fred Charles Iklé, Senator John W. Warner, Dr. Lawrence J. Korb, Lieutenant General John F. Wall, General Frederick J. Kroesen (Ret.), and Admiral Noel Gayler (Ret.).

In addition, I want to express my appreciation to panel discussants and moderators Dr. Jack Nunn, Frank J. Gaffney, Jr., Lieutenant General Brent Scowcroft (Ret.), George A. Keyworth, II, and Andrew W. Marshall and to the conference participants, who took time from their busy schedules. Working with the contributors has been an enjoyable, rewarding experience, and I appreciate their cooperation.

Special thanks are due to Major General William Burns (Ret.) for assistance in the early stages of this project, and to Ambassadors Charles Marthinson, formerly of the US Army War College, and Bruce Laingen, formerly of the National Defense University, during the conference. In addition, to Dr. Frederick T. Kiley, Director of NDU Press, to Lieutenant Colonel Paul E. Taibl, Mr. George Maerz, and Mr. Donald H. Schmoldt of the Press, and to Dr. William McCarron of East Texas State University—my gratitude for indispensable assistance in preparing this volume in its final form.

Neither this volume nor the individual articles in it should be construed to reflect the official position of the National Defense University, the Institute for National Strategic Studies, the Department of the Army, or the Department of Defense. I alone am responsible for any errors of fact or judgment.

JEFFREY SIMON
WASHINGTON, DC

Security Implications of SDI

WILL WE BE MORE SECURE IN 2010?

INTRODUCTION

A Safer Strategic Order for the Next Century

Fred Charles Iklé

All too often, supporters and critics of the present Strategic Defense Initiative (SDI) debate the issues as if they only had to be concerned about the next few years. They worry about the possible impact of SDI on the current US-Soviet arms negotiations, want to gauge the merits of SDI on the basis of short-term trade-offs under the deficit-dominated budget in the next fiscal year, or try to assess Soviet policy by taking Moscow's statements from the last three years as if that policy were the Soviet position for the next 30 years.

Every President since 1945 has been conscious that his decisions on nuclear policy and nuclear arms have an extraordinary long-term reach. Strategic offensive arms and strategic defense take some 10 years to design, develop, and build, and then, once developed, they may be deployed in our forces for another 30 years.

So each year we can effect only marginal changes in the structure and composition of our nuclear forces. If we do not today anticipate the needs of our nuclear strategy and the forces for the beginning of the next century, it will be too late. In the year 2010, for example, our President will have to confront all the risks of nuclear war and all the threats of nuclear crises with the forces that our scientists and engineers are now developing. So how can we construct the capabilities that will serve us well 20 years hence? International affairs are highly unpredictable, and this uncertainty is compounded by unforeseen developments in science and technology. Clearly, we cannot anticipate every detail. We have to be prepared for surprises, and we also have to accept that some of our work will be wasted.

We have to develop an architecture that can guide our mortar and brickwork, year after year. I believe that this task, in some ways, is akin to drafting a constitution. Our founding fathers could in no way anticipate the dynamics of our political life today or of our present national economy. Yet, the basic principles that inspired them, and the philosophers who preceded, have served our nation, and other nations under similarly constructed democratic constitutions, for hundreds of years, preserving both liberty and the functioning of self-government.

We have to write, so to speak, a constitution for our nuclear strategy. Let me try to sketch out just a few principles that would help to protect the essential purposes, yet be flexible enough—like the principles in a good constitution—to survive the vicissitudes of international affairs and changing technology:

1. First, our strategic order must serve to prevent deliberate nuclear attack. While this is an important purpose of strategy, it cannot be its only purpose. Yet, in the national nuclear strategy that prevailed until 1983, all other purposes were given short shrift. With emphasis on deterrence and retaliatory offensive forces, the strategy was designed to protect against deliberate attack. In fact, for many years the emphasis was even more narrow, focused on deterring a very large scale, or so-called "all-out" attack.

2. We have to think about a second purpose of our strategic order: to minimize the danger from an accidental or otherwise unintended initiation of nuclear attack. Obviously, deterrence is not the answer to that problem. It is precisely one of the merits of strategic defense that it can give us a means to cope with certain accidental attacks or with the unintended use of nuclear missiles.

3. A third purpose of our strategic order is that it should help reduce the sources and intensity of conflicts between the major powers, especially between the Atlantic Alliance and the Soviet Union. At the least, the strategic order should not exacerbate other sources of conflict between East and West.

It is on this third point that the pre-SDI approach and US strategy have failed badly. That approach, with its emphasis on offensive arms—on retaliation, revenge, and mutual vulnerability—has helped to perpetuate an intensely hostile East-West relationship.

Any time we think about nuclear strategy, we have to think about the utter devastation possible in the United States from a Soviet attack and similar devastation in the Soviet Union as a result of our response. This imagery is not a good seed-bed for a slowly improving understanding between East and West.

Now, these notions came about in the 1960s as we all know, because American policymakers came to believe that a relationship of mutual vulnerability might be adopted by both East and West and that this could be turned into a permanent, stable equilibrium which would be an effective basis, if not the only basis, for making progress in arms control agreements.

For those who believed in this fallacy, it became the motivating rationale for the ABM Treaty. To be sure, there was another, earlier motivation for the ABM Treaty, and that was the assessment developed in the early and mid-1960s, up to the late 1960s, that available technologies were inadequate for a missile defense. That assessment has changed, and the new technological opportunities were important for President Reagan's decision on SDI.

But the other source of this decision, as I understand it, was the inadequacy of the strategic order that would be perpetuated if we relied on the offensive dominant strategy alone.

Today I think all but a few diehards admit that the ABM Treaty did not live up to its promise. Contrary to the way in which it was advertised, the treaty did not provide the foundation for strategic stability in the sense of helping to limit the modernization, expansion, and buildup of strategic forces.

In sum, the approach prior to President Reagan's initiative on strategic defense in 1983 violated two important principles: first, it failed to provide for the risk of accidental attack, to which deterrence, almost by definition, is not an answer; and second, it failed to help reduce one of the basic sources of East-West conflict, the strategic arms competition and the fear of attack from each other.

This book addresses the transformation of our strategic order, from the present situation in which offensive

arms are totally dominant, to one in which defensive systems will play a greater, if not a dominant role. This transformation is sometimes described as dangerous, sort of
like walking on a rope over an abyss from one safe and
stable plateau to another. I believe that is a mistaken view.
We are not now on a stable plateau. In fact, for the last 20
years we have never had such stability—given the Soviet
effort of building up both offensive and defensive
strategic arms.

So we are not leaving a situation of stability as we
move toward defense; nor are we entering a situation of
instability if we do things right. Initial capabilities of defensive systems can enhance deterrence; and subsequently,
as these capabilities are augmented, they can serve to
reduce the risk of accidents and reduce the dangerous
pressures for quick uses of offensive forces that now exist,
thus further enhancing stability.

We must not forget the dangers inherent in the present situation with its pressures for quick, irreversible decisions in a nuclear crisis. I think this problem was well
illustrated in the debate between then President Reagan
and Democratic presidential candidate Walter Mondale.
Mondale argued that the Strategic Defense Initiative was a
dangerous idea. He was briefed, he said, when he
entered office, about having to push "the button"
instantly to respond to a Soviet attack, and questioned
how one could turn over such a task to SDI computers.
Of course, it's precisely the opposite point that has to be
made. It is our reliance on offensive forces and their quick
reaction that creates the nightmare that Mondale
described. Defensive systems can respond to warning
without leading to a totally catastrophic outcome.

Thus, the right view of the so-called transition is that
it is a gradual evolution providing increased defensive
capabilities that can improve our security at each step. We
don't have to cross over some dangerous gulf to reach the
promise of SDI.

To make this point a bit clearer, let me expand on it.
Not enough attention has been given to the fact that the

strategic order envisaged in the ABM treaty (assuming the ideal circumstances of the treaty rather than the way it turned out) is politically and psychologically destabilizing. By accepting the strategic order that Americans had in mind in 1972, the Soviet leaders would have had to forever place the future fate of the Soviet Union into the hands of the American leadership. Soviet leaders would have to accept indefinitely a future where any American president (or maybe even an American general) could unleash the engines of destruction that would put an end to all that Lenin built.

Whatever view of history that Soviet leaders might hold—whether it is traditional Marxist or more modern—they would not be content with this prospect. They would be unwilling to let the fate of the Soviet Union be governed, forever, by the vagaries and decisionmaking of another power—the United States today, or additional nuclear powers in the future.

In addition, a careful Soviet military observer might well have been skeptical of the US intent because of our policy for the Atlantic Alliance. That policy, as we all know, sought to combine stable, mutual vulnerability with NATO's flexible response policy. Seen from the viewpoint of a Moscow military analyst this looked like the "imperialists" were trying to go in two directions: on the one hand saying that the unleashing of nuclear war was totally deterred by the mutual deterrence relationship, but on the other proclaiming that nuclear war would be unleashed if things went badly in a defense against a conventional Soviet attack.

It is this psychological tension, a kind of doomsday tension, that is built into a strategic order relying only on offensive forces. One might predict it has a corrosive effect on East-West relations. To be sure, like any prediction in international affairs, one can not put much weight on it. Except, on this one we can look 20 years back and see that this corrosive effect, did, indeed, occur.

The Soviet strategic programs in these years—the buildup of "counterforce" missiles, active defenses, and deep underground shelters—were designed to overcome the threat from US nuclear forces. That's what Soviet force buildup was largely about. Yet, some people are again proposing we should negotiate arms control agreements to reaffirm this old approach, hoping that for some reason the leadership in Moscow would now settle down with us and become comfortable about this mad relationship that they rejected before.

Summing up, what about the "transition" to a greater role for strategic defense? I believe this transition—or evolution, as I would prefer to call it—is already under way. For one, the Soviet Union has missile defenses, both strategic and tactical, and is improving them. Second, NATO leaders now recognize that the alliance will require defenses against conventional attack, so anti-tactical ballistic missiles are being planned as an extension of NATO air defense. Third, very fundamental reasons (which I have touched on here) force the nuclear powers to prepare for a safer strategic order for the next century.

Fred Charles Iklé was Undersecretary for Policy, Department of Defense (1981-88) and Director, US Arms Control Agency (1973-77). He has been a member of the Social Science Department, RAND Corporation (1955-61) and Head of the Social Science Department (1968-73). Dr. Iklé holds an M.A. and Ph.D. from the University of Chicago, has been a research associate at Harvard Center for International Affairs (1962-63), and Professor of Political Science at the Massachusetts Institute of Technology (1964-67). Among his numerous publications are The Social Impact of Bomb Destruction *(1958),* How Nations Negotiate *(1964), and* Every War Must End *(1971).*

OVERVIEW

Jeffrey Simon

On 23 March 1983 then President Ronald Reagan announced his vision for the United States—to rid it of the threat of offensive nuclear weapons. The implications of the President's Strategic Defense Initiative (SDI) for US national security are quite profound and of potentially long-term consequence. In sum, SDI augured in a "new" defensive doctrine or way of viewing the world, requiring a radical departure in US force structure with significant consequences for security. The Strategic Defense Initiative affects US security in four broad areas: relations with the USSR; US doctrine and force structure; relations with traditional allies, specifically European NATO; and finally, continental US (CONUS) security.

This book, *Security Implications of SDI*, explores the potential long-term (in the year 2010) ramifications of SDI on US security. Divided into four parts corresponding to the general implications described above, these views offer a divergence of informed opinion. In Part IV especially, three noted experts come to markedly different conclusions in answering "Will we be more secure in the year 2010?"

Part I. Strategic Defense Initiative and Soviet Responses

Part I focuses on the general SDI program that is envisioned for the United States and what the Soviet political and military responses to such deployment are likely to be. In "US Strategic Defense in 2010: A Conjecture," Simon P. Worden speculates what US strategic defense deployments might look like in 2010. He argues that the purpose of the SDI technical program is to examine the possibility of changing deterrence from reliance on offensive nuclear weapons to greater dependence on defensive capabilities. To achieve this the SDI program has three tasks: First, it will determine whether or not survivable and cost-effective strategic systems could be deployed in the early 1990s. Second, it is determining the feasibility of the technical options that would provide defenses against new Soviet threats. Third, it will explore and develop breakthrough technologies which could extend the effectiveness of future defense systems.

Worden argues that the Anti-Ballistic Missile (ABM) systems of the 1960s suffered from defects that technology of the 1980s appears capable of solving; notably in directed energy devices, lasers and particle beams, sensors, computer technology, and operations in outer space. The SDI's multiple-layered concept for defense has the objective of finding options for at least one layer of defense during a missile's boost, midcourse, and terminal phase of flight. Initial sensor options exist for each layer: an infrared system; a long-wave infrared system; and "airborne optical systems" with ground-based "terminal imaging radars." The SDI's two basic intercept technologies are: (1) hit-to-kill non-nuclear homing interceptors; and (2) directed energy weapons including ground- and space-based lasers, space-based particle beams, and nuclear-directed energy weapons. In addition, the SDI has a program to develop a reliable battle management and communications system for its multi-layered defense concept. Finally, programs are devoted to assure survivability of defense systems, the lethality of weapons to destroy enemy ballistic missiles and warheads, and the reduction of launch costs.

The SDI "red team" is developing worst-case threat estimates and possible Soviet countermeasures which include the proliferation of current offensive weapons, new responsive offensive systems (decoys and new boosters), and methods to attack US defenses (including kinetic energy anti-satellite weapons (ASAT), nuclear explosive ASATs, and directed energy threats, such as space-based particle beams or ground-based lasers.

Worden outlines what a three-layered initial baseline defense system—that is survivable and cost effective at the margin—might look like in the 1990s. He also presents a responsive defense system which could defeat offensive threats specifically designed to defeat defenses. In sum, Worden concludes that it might not be necessary to deploy these systems. If a cooperative transition to a defense-reliant deterrent occurs, the deployed defensive system could be more modest than that necessary to defeat a worst-case offensive force.

Sayre Stevens discusses "Likely Soviet Political-Military Responses" to SDI in the next chapter. He assumes that the ABM Treaty is abrogated, Soviet efforts to halt SDI fail, and the United States deploys an operational ballistic missile defense (BMD) with space-based elements in 2000–2010. Since the United States and USSR are unable to agree upon a mutually acceptable road map, the transition to a world of defensive deterrence will not be easy and is fraught with danger and uncertainty.

Stevens argues that the Soviets perceive SDI as threatening. Politically, it threatens the USSR's superpower status achieved in SALT I and the ABM Treaty. Militarily, it threatens the reemergence of US strategic superiority. Technologically, it rekindles deep-rooted fears of US technology. Economically, it threatens needed programs for domestic economic repair. In sum, SDI threatens the Soviet belief in the dominance of the offense in countering the defense. Though the Soviets' desired response to SDI is likely to be across the wide range of forces—with active (against aerodynamic and missile threats) and passive defenses as part of the response—their ability to respond may be more constrained. Hence the Soviets will attempt to exploit political opportunities to use arms control to slow down US deployment and mount a program to solidify public support for the sacrifices that will be necessary to counter SDI.

Stevens then outlines some likely specific Soviet responses. First, overwhelming an early SDI with offensive missiles remains attractive, including more multiple independently targetable reentry vehicle (MIRVed) mobiles and follow-on systems. Also the Soviets will likely develop intercontinental ballistic missile (ICBM) countermeasures to improve penetration by developing shorter burn systems during booster and midcourse stages, complicating booster and reentry vehicle (RV) signatures, developing decoys, and fractional orbital bombardment systems (FOBS). Second, submarine-launched ballistic missiles (SLBM) follow-on systems with depressed trajectories close to the US coast also offer the Soviets attractive opportunities. Third, the Soviets will make efforts to cover a larger number of strategic targets with cruise missiles.

The Soviets are also most likely to respond to SDI with their own strategic defenses. Should erosion of the ABM Treaty occur, the USSR may capitalize on its existing advantage to field defenses. They would likely strengthen Moscow defenses and expand them to other Soviet installations; they might also establish ground- and space-based terminal defenses based on "other physical properties." In fact, Stevens expresses the concern that since the Soviets have a better ability than the United States to pursue long-term and uncertain goals, the United States might well abandon SDI at some future date only to find itself confronting a full-blown Soviet strategic defense system. This would result in a radically altered strategic balance with destabilizing effects. In sum, he feels that the foundations on which to build a full and effective strategic system is better established in the USSR than here.

Paul Nitze in "The Impact of SDI on US-Soviet Relations" notes that by the early 1990s, the SDI research program should help answer questions about the feasibility of a militarily effective, survivable, and cost-effective strategic defense. In order to better understand SDI's impact on the Soviet leadership and on relations with the United States, Nitze discusses what the Soviets have both said and done. Soviet commentary on the SDI program casts an ominous prospect on US-Soviet relations. The Soviets argue that because it represents a US effort to gain strategic superiority by gaining a first-strike capability, they are seeking to prevent an arms race in space by banning research, development, testing, and deployment of "space-strike arms," making that ban a precondition for strategic arms talks. Soviet actions, though, have not been consistent with their rhetoric. Their actions have stressed the importance of strategic defenses, they have pursued military uses of space, they have resumed arms control talks, and they have somewhat narrowed differences at negotiations. Thus, SDI and arms control are not antithetical.

Since Soviet actions suggest that their concerns and perceptions are not what they would have us believe, Nitze discusses what the Soviets *really* think. First, the Soviets want to maintain the status quo, which provides them with a superiority in conventional forces and, numerically, in prompt hard target kill capability in large ICBMs, as well as geographical advantages on the Eurasian land mass and in a centralized planning apparatus providing the capability to rapidly rechannel resources. No Soviet advantage would result from any change in the status quo. Second, though Soviet concerns about the application of exotic technologies are real, they do *not* see a hidden agenda in SDI. In other words, they understand that technologies suitable for BMD are not suitable for space-based attacks on ground targets. Finally, their lack of interest in seeking a cooperative transition up to now is understandable because it would undermine their position on "space-strike arms."

Nitze concludes with the hope that the US SDI research program will start an historic transition to a world where sophisticated technologies are applied against weapons of mass destruction rather than against people. He notes, though, that he is under no illusion that this transition will be either short or easy.

Part II. US Doctrine and Force Structure Modifications

Part II focuses on the impact that SDI will have on US doctrine and on future force structure. In "Is the Air-Defense Problem Bypassing the SDI?" Peter Wilson notes that as we develop an increasingly effective ballistic missile defense, Soviet aerodynamic attack systems will increase. The Soviets have ongoing programs including long-range air-launched and sea-launched cruise missiles (ALCM and SLCM, and supersonic versions) as well as strategic bombers (*Bear* H with AS-15s and the supersonic *Blackjack*). We should not be surprised if the Soviets greatly expand their commitment to aerodynamic threat systems.

The Soviets' interest in expanding their aerodynamic forces is substantial irrespective of early US SDI deployment. First, it helps the Soviets diversify their nuclear forces. Because Soviet fixed-ICBMs have become vulnerable since the late 1970s, their long-range bomber force and the development of ICBM mobiles (SS-25s and SS-24s) provides a hedge. Second, it supports the shift in Soviet doctrine of long non-nuclear war with NATO with need for deep-strike capabilities. Soviet long-range bombers could be used to undermine the US reinforcement of NATO, the Maritime Strategy, and also against weakened US air defenses. Third, it could be used as a bargaining chip in arms control negotiation.

Wilson argues that Gorbachev's program suggests a Soviet slow-down in military-technical competition and Soviet aerodynamic systems may be affected. Soviet options for the mid-1990s, though, might include: *Bear* H with 1000 AS-15s and *Blackjack*; a new tanker fleet, a naval version of AS-15s (the SS-N-21); and a *Backfire/Fencer* follow-on with "stealth" features. By the early 21st century, the Soviets could develop low-observable missile systems to include an advanced cruise missile follow-on to the AS-15 and an intercontinental multi-stage cruise missile on mobile ground transporters. Hence, the US Air Defense Initiative (ADI) must have surveillance and kill capabilities to defend against such threats.

Possible US ADI systems are wide and varied. For detection and tracking, the US Navy has expressed an interest in an airborne early warning airship which will nicely complement Over the Horizon Back Scatter radars; the US Air Force could invest in very-high flying TR-1 aircraft with confirmal UHF radars and C-130 aircraft with large aperture side-looking radars; and space-based radars and infrared concepts, which will require defenses against anti-satellite threats. For killing an opponent's ASAT and sensor capability, "high-brightness" directed energy weapons will need to be developed. The configuration of such systems will depend upon developments in technology, arms control, and fiscal constraints. In sum, Wilson argues that if the United States pushes ahead with strategic defenses, it will need an air defense component that may match the investment in strategic defenses significantly impacting US doctrine and force structure.

Jack Nunn, in "Supporting the Transition to a Strategic Defense," argues that making this change to a strategic defense in the United States will require overcoming significant impediments. First, the constituency for strategic defenses is small. SDI must compete with the services (Army, Air Force, and Navy) which already have large constituencies. Second, any new force mix will be constrained by what is already in place. Strategic defenses must show how their operational concepts will improve national security *before* we allocate significant resources.

Some key resource issues that will affect the change to strategic defenses include the following: First, costs are likely to be significant, but dollar estimates are premature. Second, the scientific and industrial base—the required personnel, material, and facilities—to support the transition needs to be better understood and developed. Nunn mentions, for example, the need for greater launch capabilities, propellant requirements, and optics to support strategic defense architectures and argues that the scientific and industrial transition will be as difficult as the doctrine and force structure transition.

Nunn argues that during the transition, resource trade-offs with advantages and disadvantages will exist between the differing research, development, and deployment paths chosen (e.g., early deployment or a period of extended research) and this could result in differing capabilities. Both transition paths involve scientific resource problems which require intelligent DOD planning and investment in physical plants and education of personnel to insure that the industrial base and skills will be available when required.

The ability of the US scientific and industrial base to support transition must be judged in terms of manpower, facilities, and materials. Scientific and technical manpower constraints are likely to exist in optics and artificial intelligence in the research and development (R&D) phase; and, depending on the speed of deployment, during the production and deployment phase. Key facilities appear sufficient to support extended research during R&D, though additional testing facilities may be required. Facilities sufficiency, though, will depend upon the architecture chosen and time-phasing of deployment. Some materials—which vary from raw to high technology manufactured materials—may not be available unless the government plans well in advance. Hence, Nunn argues that the United States must develop plans and sufficiently flexible resource options that will allow us to support a defense deployment.

David Emery, in "SDI and the Future," discusses SDI and the future of deterrence. He argues that, in the past, mutual deterrence was based upon the basic idea that each side must maintain roughly equal forces and equal capability to retaliate against attack. Because the USSR failed to show restraint in offensive and defensive forces and since scientific developments and emerging technologies now make new defense concepts possible, we can turn to defenses to enhance deterrence.

Though the United States and USSR realize that a balanced offense/defense mix contributes to stability, the Soviets have altered that balance by overt and covert development of defenses. SDI will restore stability. The US defensive system must be survivable, it must *not* provide incentives for Soviet proliferation, and it must assure a stable transition from our current offensive posture to one more reliant upon ballistic missile defense.

The United States has proposed that we would not deploy strategic defenses for 10 years, but would conduct research, development, and testing permitted by the ABM Treaty. After the Reykjavik talks, Gorbachev made efforts to "strengthen" the ABM Treaty in effect to restrict all laboratory testing of space elements of ABM defenses. The US goal is to seek deep reductions in strategic forces to make preemptive attack less likely. We would retain aircraft and cruise missiles to maintain deterrence and maintain defenses to prevent cheating and protect against attack from third countries. Thus, strategic defenses can enhance stability and assist and strengthen arms control.

Strategic defenses can contribute to stability by complicating surprise attack, counteracting nuclear blackmail, and re-creating a military balance. In sum, when fast first-strike systems become less effective and slower second-strike systems become dominant, world politics will be improved.

Part III. Alliance Implications

Part III focuses on SDI's impact on US alliance relationships; notably on political and military relations with the North Atlantic Treaty Organization. Arthur F. Burns and Roger P. Labrie discuss SDI's potential political

ramifications for NATO in their chapter. They argue that
the program contains elements that can either have disruptive effects on US relations with European NATO
allies or can contribute to further alliance cohesion.
Hence, the SDI program presents the United States with
an alliance management problem that, if properly managed, can contribute to US/NATO security.

European concerns about SDI surfaced early
because of the absence of consultations *before* the
March 1983 speech. Because the President did not stress
that SDI was a response to Soviet actions, Europeans
were concerned that it was an effort of the United States
to achieve superiority. In addition, by rendering nuclear
weapons obsolete, the Alliance's ultimate deterrent
would be undermined. Europeans now better understand US SDI objectives due, in part, to extensive consultations and the US invitation to participate in the
program.

SDI, though, does pose questions for the Alliance.
Ballistic missile defenses undermine NATO's traditional
strategic foundation. NATO's "flexible response" doctrine assumes rough equivalence of shared risks
between the United States and European allies. If the
United States acquires missile defenses, its risk will
become smaller, undermining the Alliance's common
risk assumption. If Europe acquires missile defenses, it
will still be vulnerable to superior Soviet/Warsaw Pact
conventional forces and tactical nuclear attack. Hence,
deterrence will be weakened, and if the Soviets develop
their defenses, it threatens to undermine the British and
French nuclear deterrent. Finally, some Europeans view
SDI as an economic threat; they fear the technological
gap between the United States and Europe will widen as
a result of the program.

Burns and Labrie argue that as an Alliance leader,
the United States must guide the difficult transition from
an offense-dominant to a defense-dominant strategic
environment. Though the authors have no answer as to
how to achieve this, they posit some guiding principles.

In the transition, the United States must: (1) maximize close consultation with allies; (2) achieve equal levels of protection for the United States and Europe at each level of deployment (including eliminating disparities in conventional forces and chemical weapons); (3) encourage the greatest amount of allied cooperation and participation as possible; and (4) continue to push for arms control measures.

In "Implications of SDI for NATO's Conventional Force Posture," Franz-Joseph Schulze discusses the potential impact of SDI on NATO's conventional force posture. He starts with the assumption that, during the period of transition, SDI technological breakthroughs will strengthen NATO's conventional defense. He argues that even an imperfect defense will enhance strategic deterrence because it will deprive the aggressor of the required certainty and discourage temptations to launch a nuclear first-strike.

To date, we have not yet secured arms control agreements that have brought about a reduction in strategic nuclear weapons because they were based on the concept of Mutual Assured Destruction (MAD). The need to secure the capability to destroy the aggressor in retaliation has led to the tendency for both sides to increase the quantity and quality of nuclear weapons. Schulze feels, though, that SDI creates some new chances for arms control. In addition, if the Nitze criterion of "favorable marginal cost" of defensive systems is followed, then both sides will have an incentive to cut down offensive potential.

The Soviets never adopted MAD; instead, they have stressed damage limitation through passive protection and active defenses (anti-ballistic missiles around Moscow and air defense). Not only have the Soviets tested their air defense against ballistic missiles, but if they expanded it to include an anti-tactical ballistic missile (ATBM) capability, European security would be greatly affected and Europe *must* respond. Strengthening NATO's capabilities to counter the Soviet/Warsaw

Pact conventional superiority is an urgent priority for *all* NATO members, Schulze argues. NATO can strengthen its conventional force posture considerably by exploiting its technological superiority better than it has traditionally.

The findings of SDI research might contribute substantially to the rapid development and deployment of modern conventional systems, particularly conventionally-armed ballistic missiles to neutralize Warsaw Pact air forces and to delay, disrupt, and destroy follow-on forces. NATO must upgrade its capability to minimize the probability of surprise. These improvements include all-weather surveillance, target-acquisition capabilities, close links between national and NATO intelligence systems, the coordinated evaluation of intelligence, real-time data transmission, and barrier and denial measures. NATO also needs to upgrade its integrated air defense system in order to neutralize the improved accuracy of the Warsaw Pact's ballistic, cruise, and stand-off missile systems. The results of SDI research could have great relevance for the buildup of an improved European air defense system.

In sum, Schulze feels that the technological breakthroughs needed to successfully implement SDI will contribute greatly to the strengthening of NATO's conventional defenses, and will do so much earlier than expected. For example, progress in sensor technology and signal processing could provide conventional forces with effective real-time target acquisition; progress in the broad field of "Search, Acquisition, Tracking, and Kill Assessment" (SATKA) could serve European air (as well as missile) defense; and electro-magnetic guns could revolutionize the anti-armor battle. Hence, close cooperation between Western Europe and the United States in SDI research, as well as in strengthening the conventional defense in Europe, would be a striking demonstration of NATO's solidarity.

Part IV. Will We Be More Secure in 2010?

Part IV includes three essays by well-known specialists who arrive at very different conclusions regarding the impact of SDI on US security. *Robert Komer* argues that the SDI program will probably undermine US security in 2010. He feels that the program will probably end up making non-nuclear war more feasible at a time when the enormous costs of doing so will seriously reduce US capabilities for deterring or fighting conventional wars. Since the Soviets are likely to match US strategic defense developments, their superiority in most non-nuclear capabilities (except at sea) particularly around the Eurasian rimlands will likely undermine the effectiveness of extended US deterrence. In essence, this nuclear deterrence, which has provided a security umbrella around the world, will be reduced, making Eurasia more vulnerable to the USSR.

While the United States and its allies (specifically European NATO and Japan) have the ability to match Soviet conventional superiority in peacetime; they have not demonstrated the will, nor are they likely to do so in the future. Thus, making the United States and its allies safe from nuclear devastation will come at the cost of increasing the likelihood of conventional war. The trillion dollar cost projections for SDI-type programs will also make the United States and its allies less capable of coping with conventional conflicts. In short, the costs of SDI may make it exceedingly difficult to deter conventional war; removing the United States' extended deterrent umbrella will make its allies more vulnerable, ironically at a time when this country will be even more dependent on these allies for coalition defense.

In sum, Komer feels that the United States will probably be in a materially more difficult security situation in 2010; the current comparatively stable strategic order of nuclear standoff would become less stable and more volatile if conventional war risks and costs again become dominant. Hence, the "cure" of SDI might be worse than controlling the "disease" of current strategic nuclear parity.

Albert Gore expresses mixed feelings about SDI. He argues that what passes for "safety" is really "stability" which is either a mutual condition or nonexistent. Either the US and USSR find themselves relatively at ease on the question of the first-strike capabilities of the other, or *both* countries are involved in an unstable relationship. According to Gore, there are two paths to mutual stability—defense dominance (Star Wars) or offense dominance (deterrence).

The US transition to a defensively dominant strategic environment is fraught with danger. Long before we reach a state of "mutual assured survival" through defenses, we would reach a destabilized state of what Gore calls "splendid first-strike capability"—the means to attack the enemy's nuclear forces and then use defenses to sop up his disorganized response.

Gore argues that it is essential that the United States continue to rely upon offensive systems for deterrence and defense. Though stability can exist at lower levels of offenses (which can be achieved through arms control), progressively lower levels can be unstable. Modernization of offensive systems—particularly mobile ICBMs— are the key to stable nuclear relationships.

Gore postulates a strategy for US security that is based upon mutual stability. In conjunction with vigorous research of defense systems, we should stay within SALT limits, which is a bridge to a safer future, taking reductions in such a way that we retain the most survivable warheads for the longest period of time. Specifically, we should *not* dismantle Poseidons early on; we should take our cuts from a mix of older systems such as Titan and Polaris (or Minuteman III). In sum, we can substantially increase survivable SLBM warheads in our forces until more highly survivable, follow-on systems (Midgetman, Stealth, and more Tridents) become available.

If we destroy the Strategic Arms Limitation Talks (SALT) and the ABM Treaty, the world of 2010 will be more dangerous. Stability can be retained, he states, *if* both sides introduce mobile ICBMs under controlled conditions that keep the SALT framework intact. If we can bargain down to mutual and verifiable constraints on SDI research which permit vigorous programs to continue—but reinforce barriers against development and deployment—then the world of 2010 will, indeed, have safer stability.

Eugene V. Rostow comes to very different conclusions regarding SDI's impact on US security. Rostow argues that it is essential to develop strategic defense systems to enhance US security. Assuming that the USSR does not change its behavior and that the United States continues to recognize that domination of the Eurasian land mass by a single power would be detrimental to US security, coalition defense will remain critical to US security in 2010.

Rostow argues that the United States and USSR maintain two completely different views of nuclear deterrence. The US goal is to deter Soviet *offensive* aggression against our interests; the Soviet, to deter an American *defense* against Soviet aggression. Hence, particularly since SALT I and the ABM Treaty in 1972, the USSR has been seeking nuclear superiority in ground-based systems and strategic defenses. Their goal is to seek a plausible first-strike capability to achieve victory without war.

The United States must eliminate the Soviet first-strike capability. This only can be achieved by a crash offensive weapons building program, and developing defensive weapons forcing the USSR to use 80–90 (rather than 25–30) percent of its nuclear forces in first-strike, or an arms agreement based on the principle of US-USSR deterrent retaliatory equality. Unfortunately, the USSR has held to the principle of equal reductions, *not* reductions to equal levels.

Rostow believes that SDI can help restore the nuclear balance since conventional forces alone cannot protect the Eurasian land mass from domination. He argues that SDI is "misnamed"; it should be Strategic Defense Response as it is really a *response* to Soviet strategic defense developments since 1972. By 2010 the United States must stabilize the offensive-defensive arms relationship with the USSR. This must be achieved through cooperative SDI efforts with our allies and with the Soviets; we must share awareness (not technology) of what each other is doing. Successful development of US ballistic missile defenses should make it easier for this country to eliminate the threat of a first-strike capability; and by doing so the West will restore the vitality of collective security in the Atlantic, Pacific, and the Middle East.

In sum, three well-known US security policy experts express three different perspectives on the impact of SDI on US security and whether or not various aspects of defensive doctrine should be adopted or elements of defensive systems deployed.

Jeffrey Simon is a Senior Fellow in the Strategic Capabilities Assessment Center, Institute for National Strategic Studies, National Defense University. Previously he was Chief, National Military Strategy Branch and Soviet Threat Analyst at the Strategic Studies Institute, US Army War College. He has taught at Georgetown University and has held research positions at System Planning Corporation, the RAND Corporation, and the American Enterprise Institute. Among his publications are Ruling Communist Parties and Detente (Washington, DC: American Enterprise Institute, 1975), Cohesion and Dissension in Eastern Europe: Six Crises (New York: Praeger, 1983), Warsaw Pact Forces: Problems of Command and Control (Boulder: Westview 1985), Security Implications of Nationalism in Eastern Europe (Boulder: Westview, 1986), and NATO-Warsaw Pact Force Mobilization (Washington, DC: National Defense University Press, 1988). Dr. Simon holds a Ph.D from the University of Washington and an M.A. from the University of Chicago.

PART I

STRATEGIC DEFENSE INITIATIVE
and
SOVIET RESPONSES

US STRATEGIC DEFENSES IN 2010: A CONJECTURE

Simon P. Worden

To extrapolate current information and project the strategic environment in 25 years is extremely difficult, particularly in the case of strategic defense. Its role in our future deterrent relationship will depend on many factors including arms control, Soviet strategic objectives and force deployments, and the US political situation. This problem can be bounded in two ways.

First, President Reagan's objective, involving a cooperative transition to a defense-reliant deterrent, sets basic Strategic Defense Initiative (SDI) goals. The form of strategic defenses in this case will depend on the level and kind of cooperative agreements reached with the Soviet Union. To help reach this more stable deterrent relationship, the United States must prove that defenses can be effective against an unconstrained and hostile Soviet Union. Second, while the United States might have to prove such defenses are feasible to persuade the Soviet Union to enter a cooperative transition to a defense-reliant deterrent relationship, the actual defenses deployed in the transition may be far more modest than those studied in the worst-case analyses.

The SDI technical program is part of a national effort to examine the possibility of changing deterrence from reliance on offensive nuclear weapons to greater dependence on defensive capabilities. Advancing our technology base and establishing capabilities for effective ballistic missile defense can complement our efforts to obtain significant and verifiable reductions in offensive nuclear forces. The SDI is structured to contribute to these goals in three ways: One, it will provide a technology base for possible future strategic defenses to enhance the security of the United States and its allies. Two, the program will provide the data for decisions in the early 1990s on whether or not (and if so, what kind) of future strategic defense deployment is feasible.

Three, effective defenses would eliminate cheating which today undermines arms control and would become even more prevalent with low levels of nuclear weapons.

At the same time effective defenses would dramatically increase incentives for easing back on offensive nuclear forces by greatly reducing—or eliminating—the military utility of ballistic missiles.

To support the national objective of moving to a defense-reliant strategic regime, the SDI program will perform three tasks: One, it will determine whether or not survivable and cost-effective strategic defense systems could be deployed in the 1990s. Meeting such criteria will ensure that defenses would, indeed, contribute to security and stability. In the short term, SDI would serve as a hedge against unilateral Soviet attempts to deploy nationwide defenses in violation of the ABM Treaty; in the longer term, it would be a basis for a possible mutual transition to a defense-reliant strategic relationship. Two, the SDI is attempting to determine the feasibility of technical options that would provide effective defensive systems against potential new Soviet offensive threats that might be specifically designed to defeat US defenses. These new offensive threats are referred to as "responsive" since they are postulated Soviet responses to the US program. Three, the SDI will explore and develop breakthrough technologies which could extend the effectiveness of future defensive systems. While these innovative technologies may not be required to begin a transition to an improved deterrent relationship, they would move us toward our goal of eliminating nuclear war.

SDI Technologies

Technology of the 1960s and 1980s. Anti-Ballistic Missile (ABM) systems designed by both the United States and the Soviet Union in the 1960s suffered from numerous technical defects. First, those ABM systems were only capable of operating in the final few minutes of a ballistic missile's flight. The attacker thus had more time to structure an attack to defeat the defenses. Second, those systems relied on large, nuclear-armed interceptor missiles. Not only were these interceptors costly, but the nuclear interceptor warhead could produce side-effects, damaging to *both* the defended targets on the ground and other vital military systems. Third, the ABM systems relied on a small number of large radar sensor facilities which were themselves vulnerable and represented a potential Achilles heel. Finally, 1960s' management and computer capabilities could not handle the large number of missile "decoys" and other countermeasures designed to defeat the defense.

The technology of the 1980s, however, appears to provide solutions to all of these problems. First, directed energy devices, lasers, and particle beams may make it possible to intercept and destroy nuclear warheads from very great distances at or near the speed of light (300,000 kilometers per second). These directed energy technologies not only show particular promise for performing missile intercept early in the missile's flight, but they can more effectively discriminate warheads from decoys and other material designed to confuse a defensive system. Second, new sensors, possibly using infrared or visible light rather than radar beams alone, are rapidly becoming feasible. Such sensors can help detect, track, and identify attacking objects from the moment they are launched. These sensors can also be based on small mobile platforms, thus reducing their vulnerability. Third, progress in computer technology is yielding defensive systems capable of handling a defensive engagement against many hundreds of thousands of attacking objects. Fourth, by combining new sensor technologies with micro-miniaturized computers, extremely small non-nuclear interceptor missiles (called "kinetic energy weapons") can be constructed. These missiles would destroy their targets by colliding with them rather than by detonating a nuclear warhead nearby. Also, because of their small size, such missiles are likely to be much less costly than the older nuclear-armed ABM missiles.

Finally, the United States is entering an era of greatly expanded access to outer space. The ability to operate in, and routinely access outer space, makes new concepts for effective strategic defenses appealing.

Multiple-Layered Defense Concept. The objective of the SDI is to discover and employ technologies for intercepting the missile soon after it is launched and before its payload of multiple reentry vehicles is fully deployed—and to have many different intercept opportunities throughout the missile's flight. In each defensive layer, systems must be defined which would first detect a missile attack, define missile targets, and identify individual threatening objects. Next, defensive weapons must be pointed and directed at the ballistic missile or warhead targets. Finally, a battle management system must handle each phase of the battle reliably, and hand on unintercepted targets to subsequent layers.

Although current ballistic missiles typically have three distinct phases of flight (boost, midcourse, and terminal phases), future ballistic missile threats may have significantly altered phases. Our objective is to find options for employing at least one layer of defense in each phase. The important aspect of a multi-layered defense is not whether the layers correspond to typical ballistic missile flight phases, but whether each layer is effective and independent from other layers. Thus, if the Soviets shorten the boost phase to confound a defense operating primarily during that phase, the SDI multi-layered defense would immediately respond to the next level of missile flight. Additional Soviet countermeasures would impose prohibitive weight, cost, and performance penalties on the Soviets.

Sensor Programs. Initial sensor options exist for at least three independent layers. (1) For an initial boost phase defense, an advanced infrared sensor system—a

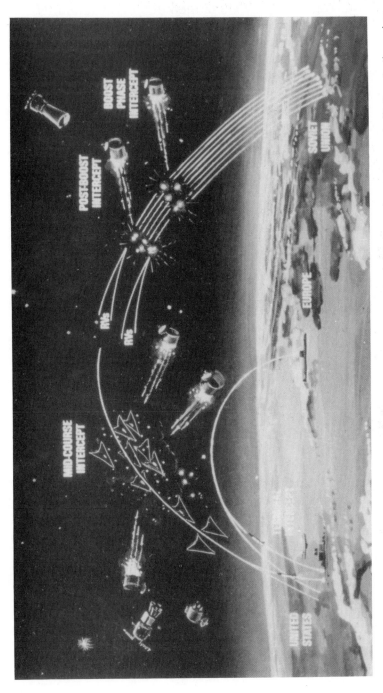

Multiple-Layered Defense. Shown are phases of a ballistic missile flight for an intercontinental-range ballistic missile and an intermediate-range ballistic missile. The longer-range missile has four phases: boost, post-boost (which may be considered an extension of boost phase), midcourse, and terminal. Shorter-range missiles usually carry only one warhead and may not have a post-boost phase.

follow-on to the current US launch detection satellites placed at geostationary altitudes—can identify and track boosters. (2) For intercept during post-boost and mid-course phases outside the earth's atmosphere, the sensing function becomes more difficult because the sensors must be able to track the relatively "cold" post-boost vehicle and warheads, and must provide accurate state (trajectory and position) vectors to weapons systems. Long-wave infrared sensors located at mid-altitude orbits can perform this function. (3) For late midcourse and terminal phase intercept, two different sensor concepts exist. In the first, a set of "optical" subsystems consisting of various infrared and laser-ranging sensors would be carried on an airborne platform to perform tracking and discrimination functions. Such "airborne optical systems" might ultimately be carried on high altitude unmanned aircraft. A second sensor option, which could ultimately be used in conjunction with the first, might be a series of ground-based "terminal imaging radars." These radars would discriminate warheads from decoys outside the atmosphere by forming an image of a potential threat object.

In addition, the SDI sensor program includes a number of technology efforts. For example, programs exist to collect data on current Soviet warheads, develop new infrared sensors, and devise long-lived cryogenic coolers for use in space. The programs include advanced technologies for obtaining images of potential threat objects to discriminate warheads from decoys, using synthetic aperture laser- or radar-imaging techniques. US capabilities to acquire detailed images of deployed warheads and decoys during post-boost phase, and images of potential threat objects during midcourse, make the construction of credible and low-cost Soviet decoys very difficult.

Intercept Technology. Two basic types of intercept technology are included in the SDI: (1) hit-to-kill non-nuclear homing interceptors (a form of kinetic energy weapon) can be deployed for intercept in every phase of a ballistic missile's flight. This basic intercept technology was demonstrated in the successful Homing Overlay Experiment (HOE) in June 1984; (2) Directed energy weapons, lasers, and particle beams allow a defensive system to respond instantly to an attack, and can be employed during all phases of a ballistic missile's flight. Kinetic energy weapons could be used for boost-phase intercept, since small rocket-powered homing interceptors could be carried on a satellite. The same space-based interceptors could also operate during the midcourse phase.

Similarly, ground-based kinetic energy weapons, with interceptor vehicles similar to the space-based interceptors, can intercept warheads in space (e.g., "exo-atmospherically"). A different type of interceptor system could operate inside the atmosphere (e.g., "endo-atmospherically"), for terminal defense at altitudes between 10-30 kilometers. For these terminal interceptors, a non-nuclear warhead would be guided to the vicinity of its warhead target by a series of external commands and on-board infrared sensors. The interceptor would maneuver to within a few meters of the target and discharge a small pellet cloud which would then destroy the target.

In the longer run, a potential aggressor may choose to construct so-called fast-burn boosters to minimize their vulnerability to boost-phase weapons. One SDI response would be to develop kinetic interceptors with higher velocities to reach the ballistic missile target despite its shortened boost time. While rocket-propelled interceptors are currently limited to velocities of about 10 km/sec or less, velocities approaching 20 km/sec or greater might be needed to intercept fast-burn boosters. The new technology of hyper-velocity launchers offers options for these higher velocities. These devices accelerate projectiles electrically rather than explosively as in a gun or rocket.

Directed Energy Weapons. Directed energy weapons include lasers (which could destroy a missile by burning a hole in a warhead or missile) and particle

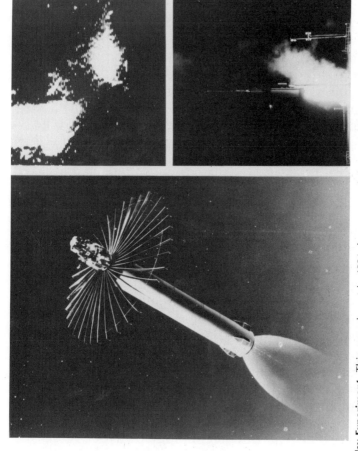

The Homing Overlay Experiment. This experiment in 1984 demonstrated that a "bullet" can hit a "bullet." Further technological progress in this concept offers the hope of a survivable and cost-effective non-nuclear ballistic missile defense operating in both boost and midcourse phases. The photo at the lower right shows the target ICBM warhead being fired from Vandenburg Air Force Base in California. The interceptor, shown in an artist's conception at the left, scored a direct hit over 100 miles up in space as the warhead arched toward the Kwajalein Missile Range in the Pacific Ocean. The photo in the upper right depicts the direct hit scored by the interceptor.

beams, containing individual atoms or charged particles moving at velocities near to the speed of light (which can penetrate deep inside a target and destroy or disrupt its internal workings). Four possible types of directed energy weapons are under consideration: ground-based lasers, space-based lasers, space-based particle beams, and nuclear-directed energy weapons.

(1) Ground-based lasers direct a high quality laser beam up through the atmosphere; and space mirrors relay the beam to the ballistic missile or warhead targets. The SDI program envisions three major parts of this concept. First, the ground-based laser itself must be a short-wave laser system to keep the size of the space-based relay mirrors small (e.g., a few meters or less in diameter). The SDI is investigating two types of lasers (excimer and free electron) for this function. Second, we must demonstrate that the beam can be sent into space without being distorted by the atmosphere. Third, we must validate the relay mirror technology.

(2) Lasers can also be placed in space. We have already demonstrated that infrared lasers with megawatts of continuous power are feasible on the ground. In a test during August 1985, the megawatt-class Mid-Infrared Advanced Chemical Laser (MIRACL) laser at White Sands, New Mexico showed that even modest levels of laser power are very lethal against current ballistic missile boosters. However, because chemical lasers like the MIRACL produce infrared light, numerous large mirrors must be phased together to produce suitably bright space-based lasers for ballistic missile defense. Efforts in the space-based laser area will concentrate on this problem.

(3) Work on particle beams focuses on neutral particle hydrogen atom beams. Since hydrogen atoms are electrically neutral, they will not be diverted by the earth's magnetic field. Several constellations of 10 space-based neutral particle beam weapons could defeat many thousands of ballistic missiles and tens of thousands of nuclear warheads in space.

Lethality Test of the MIRACL Laser. The Mid-Infrared Advanced Chemical Laser (MIRACL) was tested against a booster rocket under simulated launch conditions, at White Sands, New Mexico. The booster first-stage (at left) was loaded with water to simulate fuel, and weights were placed on the top to produce gravitational acceleration stresses like those the booster would experience in flight. This experiment helped US researchers to determine the amount of laser energy needed to destroy ballistic missiles in flight.

(4) All of the above directed energy concepts derive their energy from either chemical reactions or electrical power. Another directed energy idea is an X-ray laser, which would be powered by a small nuclear-explosive device. Although the SDI is focused on non-nuclear options, the Department of Energy is investigating nuclear-directed energy concepts as a hedge to possible Soviet breakthroughs in this area and to explore all possible defensive options.

Battle Management. The United States is devoting considerable attention to the question of whether suitably reliable battle management and communications systems can be constructed for a multi-layered defense system. Experts estimate that tens of millions of lines of computer code would be needed for such a system, with data computation rates of about a billion calculations per second. The United States has state-of-the-art hardware capable of this processing rate, but software development methods do not yet provide the necessary sophistication. At current software-development it would take thousands of people 10 years or more to generate the necessary software. Thus, the SDI organization is investigating new methods to automate software production and check-out.

Survivability and Lethality. In addition to battle management work, a fifth SDI program is devoted to survivability, lethality, and related key technologies. Survivability simply means assessing methods to ensure survivability of defensive systems and elements, particularly space-based portions. The lethality program is directed toward understanding the exact performance parameters, particularly for directed energy weapons, needed to confidently destroy ballistic missiles and warheads.

Two key technologies are also being pursued. Today, it costs several thousand dollars per kilogram to launch material to low-earth orbit on the space shuttle. Present systems architecture studies show that launch cost alone could dominate overall system costs, unless the cost-to-orbit is severely reduced. The SDI has a program to work with NASA and other DOD offices to develop these space "logistics" technologies. In a similar vein, system analyses show that we may need burst electrical power in space of several tens of megawatts and continuous power of up to a megawatt. The SDI program includes both non-nuclear and nuclear-reactor approaches.

Soviet Threat Evolution

It is extremely difficult to estimate the size and character of the Soviet threat in the years ahead. Nonetheless, an SDI "red team" is charged with developing credible worst-case threat estimates and possible Soviet countermeasures to a defensive system. Responsive threats fall into three general categories: (1) proliferation of current offensive systems; (2) construction of new, responsive Soviet offensive forces; and (3) development of methods to attack US defensive systems.

1. *Proliferation of Current Systems.* If the Soviet Union continues to expand its offensive forces at the same rate as the past decade, it could have an offensive force of 30-40,000 warheads by 2010.* Thus, a baseline US defensive system must counter this increased threat in a manner which is cost-effective at the margin.

2. *New Offensive Systems.* Responsive offensive systems generally take one of two forms: decoys and new boosters. One new Soviet offensive direction would be to develop and deploy substantial numbers of decoys in midcourse phase. Hence, a responsive US defensive system must be able to handle up to several hundred thousand lightweight decoys. While current Soviet offensive missiles probably could be modified to deploy substantial numbers of decoys in the next

---

Soviet Military Power, 1986 (Washington, DC: Government Printing Office, 1986).

decade or so, in the longer run, new booster systems could be developed to degrade the boost-phase defensive layer. Since it takes the United States at least a decade to develop, test, and begin deployment of new offensive missiles—assuming a similar time scale for the Soviet Union—the USSR is unlikely to develop and deploy a completely new generation of offensive missiles until after 2000.

Two approaches might be tried for a Soviet responsive booster. The first approach would be to shorten boost time to minimize vulnerability to boost-phase defensive systems. Current Soviet missiles have boost times from a few minutes to over five minutes. Post-boost deployment of warheads takes several additional minutes. However, while Soviet boost-time could be shortened to less than a minute in a new "fast-burn booster," deployment of multiple warheads must wait until the missile has risen above most of the atmosphere to maintain accuracy and deploy credible decoys. A fast-burn booster would be able to burn out before rocket-propelled kinetic energy weapons could reach the booster. Further, the fast-burn booster would be shielded by the atmosphere from neutral particle beams and nuclear-directed energy weapons which do not penetrate deeply into the atmosphere. It does not appear feasible to construct a large fast-burn booster with a payload comparable to the SS-18, the heavy ICBM which is the current mainstay of Soviet offensive forces. A second Soviet approach might be an attempt to shield offensive missiles against some kinds of lasers. How much shielding can reasonably be added to a missile or how much protection might be provided are unclear. However, the combination of laser shielding, fast-burn features, and decoys would reduce the total Soviet throw-weight by a large factor.

3. *Methods to Attack US Defenses.* As a prelude to a first strike, the Soviet Union might choose to pursue ways to destroy US defenses. To achieve the required level of survivability, a defensive system need not be invulnerable, but it must maintain a sufficient degree of

effectiveness to fulfill its mission, even in the face of determined attacks against it. In addition, survivable defensive systems must cost less than the defense suppression measures an opponent might use against them.

Three types of threats to space-based elements could come into play: kinetic energy anti-satellite weapons (ASAT), nuclear explosive ASATs, and directed-energy threats, such as space-based particle beams or ground-based lasers. Satellites can be hardened against nuclear attack to a degree that a direct nuclear hit would be needed to destroy them. Shielding also appears feasible against lasers and particle beams. Such shielding could be effective against even advanced directed-energy threats which might not exist for many decades. While shielding can be added to offensive missiles and warheads to protect them as well, it is easier to progressively shield a spacecraft by repeated deliveries of material from the ground, while an offensive missile must do its job in a single launch. Since each missile has only limited excess payload for shielding, there is a stringent limit in how well the missile and its payload can be shielded. In sum, an ability to repeatedly and affordably deliver mass to space means that defensive satellites could be made far more survivable than the missiles and warheads they would be designed to defeat.

The importance of low-cost and reliable means of delivering payloads to orbit, including shielding, underscores the survivability requirements. One of the highest priority SDI programs is the space logistics effort. Options being examined include the Space Shuttle, new heavy lift unmanned vehicles derived from it, new expendable or reusable launch vehicles, and the so-called "spaceplane."

Both nuclear and non-nuclear ASATs may be countered through a combination of maneuvering and, possibly, enforcement of a self-defense zone, using the same kinetic energy interceptors envisioned for missile defense as self-defense weapons. A similar cost-exchange advantage should exist for ground-based ASAT attackers, since a ground-launched ASAT requires as sophisticated and costly a launch system as a nuclear offensive warhead. Sensor satellites with vulnerable optical elements may be placed at sufficiently high altitudes that they would be both difficult to detect and difficult to attack. Moreover, these sensor satellites could also be defended by escort kinetic energy interceptors. Analysis has shown that if it is cheaper to preposition mass in space than it is to launch it from the ground on a rocket, then all methods of survivability (maneuver, deception, armoring, and self-defense) favor the defense of prepositioned defensive elements.

Ground- and air-based survivability also is essential. Mobile air-based and ground-based sensors would be difficult to locate and destroy. The dispersal and possible mobility of interceptors would similarly enhance survival prospects. Since a multi-layered defensive system has boost and midcourse defensive layers, it would be difficult for an aggressor to calculate the force levels necessary to destroy those ground-based elements which lie behind the first defensive layers. The fact that a successful preemptive attack must first destroy each layer of a defensive system in turn greatly decreases the aggressor's confidence in a successful attack.

Initial Baseline And Responsive Defensive Systems

Initial defensive systems must meet the criteria of survivability and cost effectiveness at the margin. In the previous section, I described how defensive systems could be made survivable. To see how they could be cost effective, I will now outline one possible defensive system concept, feasible for deployment during the 1990s.

This defensive system could have three defensive layers. For the boost-phase defense, thousands of

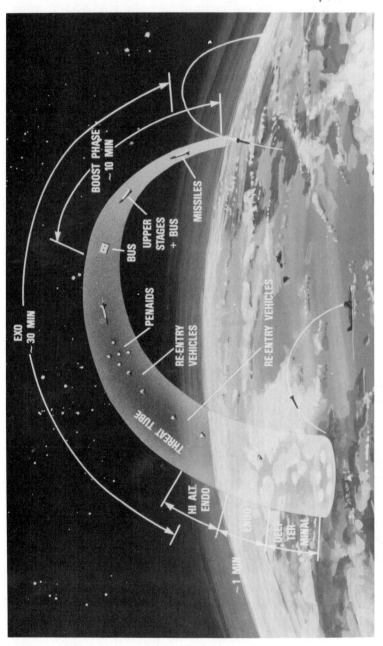

Baseline System. Although many initial system architectures are feasible for the mid- to late-1990s, the one shown above places our efforts in context. Strategic defense systems have three main functional elements: weapons, sensors, and battle management. SDI research includes at least one option for each function for at least three independent defensive layers.

rocket-powered homing interceptors would be carried on several hundred satellite carriers, each holding tens of interceptors. A boost-phase surveillance and tracking system deep in space would provide attack warning and booster track information. These same systems could operate in boost phase and also post-boost phase for the multiple warhead systems.

During midcourse, a space-based kinetic energy system has at least one additional intercept opportunity. Additional sensors, which can track perhaps hundreds of thousands of objects and discriminate warheads from decoys, are needed to conduct the midcourse battle. A network of infrared sensor platforms, perhaps ten or less satellites in all placed in intermediate altitude orbits, would precisely locate and discriminate decoys from warheads and track all potential targets during the midcourse phase.

The midcourse phase provides additional opportunities for both warhead interception and discrimination of warheads from decoys. Ground-based exo-atmospheric interceptors can be committed to attack a target while potential targets are still in early midcourse flight. After the first midcourse intercept attempt, midcourse sensors can assess the outcome and commit another wave of interceptors for those cases where the first intercept attempt failed. Since each ground-based interceptor site can defend an area of several thousand kilometers diameter, a few sites would be sufficient for either Europe or the United States.

A terminal layer provides an additional intercept opportunity within the atmosphere at altitudes between 10-30 kilometers. At these high altitudes even attacking warheads, which have been "salvage-fused" to detonate when intercepted, will be unable to damage unhardened sites on the ground such as cities or large military bases.

Two different sensor concepts described earlier might provide complementary coverage for late midcourse and terminal defense. In the first, a set of "optical" subsystems consisting of various infrared and laser-ranging sensors would be carried on an airborne platform to perform tracking and discrimination functions. Since each airborne sensor system could perform the required sensor function for an area of 1,000 kilometers diameter or more, only a few would be needed for all of Western Europe. The second sensor option, ground-based "Terminal Imaging Radars," could begin discriminating warheads from decoys outside the atmosphere by forming an image of a potential threat object. The smaller "footprint" of coverage for the radars makes them best suited for defense of high-priority targets such as missile fields, command, control, and communications (C^3) sites, and military staging areas.

Terminal interceptor missiles would be distributed over many sites, with only a few missiles per site. Dispersal, and possibly mobility of sensors and interceptors, could make terminal systems highly survivable. In addition to the "strategic" possibilities described here, work is proceeding on an "underlay" defense for use on the battlefield against the shortest range ballistic missiles. These interceptors would operate below 15 kilometers altitude and would either use a "hit-to-kill" warhead like the terminal interceptors described above or could use a small nuclear charge, which would be an effective response against salvage-fused attackers. Though their single kiloton-class nuclear warheads would be small enough to cause little or no damage on the ground, they would effectively disrupt the large attacking warhead before it could detonate.

An interesting finding of SDI analyses to date is that boost- and space-based midcourse systems postulated for the defense of the United States appear to be oversized for the defense of Western Europe.

The dominant requirement for midcourse defense is decoy discrimination. Since atmospheric drag prevents the deployment of decoys within the atmosphere, and only the longest-range missiles threatening Europe, such as the SS-20s, spend the predominant share of their flight time outside the atmosphere, the decoy problem is non-existent for many threats to Europe. Even for the SS-20, payloads are much less than for intercontinental missiles, leaving little excess payload for decoys.

Although the shortest-range missiles never leave the atmosphere and thus cannot be detected by currently feasible space-based kinetic energy interceptors, these missiles have much lower velocities than intermediate—and intercontinental—range missiles. Thus, terminal interceptors can detect and intercept them throughout most of their flight. (The longer-range SS-20s and SS-22s are vulnerable to space-based and boost-phase weapons.) The limitations on intercepting shorter-range missiles are offset by the smaller number of warheads and missiles involved.

Soviet missile attacks against targets in Europe probably would occur over a much longer time than an ICBM attack on the United States and probably would involve a smaller number of missiles and warheads, giving the defense time to bring far more of its assets into play than in a mass Intercontinental Ballistic Missile (ICBM) attack. Indeed, ground-based systems alone appear adequate to defeat current threats to Europe. However, if these ground-based systems are complemented with space-based defensive layers, they will provide a strong hedge against potential Soviet moves to redirect longer-range systems (such as ICBMs) against Europe to counter the ground-based defenses.

Among the most important features of future defensive systems are the battle management and communications systems. Although much of the focus of public discussion has been on weapons, the character of future defensive systems will be largely driven by the type of battle management architecture chosen. A distributed control system with a centralized mode control seems the most effective and survivable approach. Individual sub-elements of the defensive system would be responsible for all defensive activities within a certain geographical zone and could operate independently from other zones. However, the defensive "mode"— including alert status, thresholds for defensive actions, and degree of autonomy—would be keyed to a central defensive control system. A central mode control permits man to remain "in-the loop."

An accurate cost estimate for the system described above is impossible at this time. However, rough cost-estimates for multi-layered defensive systems of this type range from tens to hundreds of billions of dollars. More important than the basic system costs are the costs at the margin to enhance the defensive system in response to proliferating offensive threats. We can reasonably assume that the Soviet offensive forces cost an amount comparable to US forces. Even highly MIRV'd systems like the MX cost in the range of 20-30 million dollars to deploy per warhead. In the face of a three-layer system of moderate effectiveness (such as that described above), the Soviets would have to add hundreds of thousands of warheads at a cost equivalent to trillions of dollars to preserve their present ability to destroy several thousand US military targets in a first strike. The additional cost of kinetic energy defensive interceptors is unknown at the present time. However, the SDI goal is less than one million dollars per interceptor, whether space-based or ground-based. Since these missiles might be comparable in size and complexity to current surface- or air-to-air missiles which cost several hundred thousand dollars or less per missile, the SDI goal is certainly reasonable.

As discussed earlier, the Soviet Union might try to develop sophisticated decoys in the late 1990s and beyond. For this reason the SDI is investigating options for "interactive discrimination" using first-generation directed-energy devices, particle beams, or lasers. For example, moderate power laser pulses can strike a potential threat object and cause it to recoil. Heavy objects, presumably warheads, would recoil only slightly compared to a lightweight decoy, thereby identifying the heavy warhead as a threatening object. The neutral particle beam offers another option for interactive discrimination. Space-based neutral particle beams produce nuclear radiation which is proportional to the mass of an object. Thus, the level of radiation produced by a particle beam striking an object in space can reveal whether the object is a heavy warhead or a lightweight decoy. A small number of particle beam devices placed in space, along with associated sensors, could defeat Soviet attempts to deploy numerous lightweight decoys. If the decoy problem is solved in this manner, it might be possible to completely stop a very large attack using the existing space-based kinetic energy interceptor system discussed above. Thus, even if the Soviet Union developed a new generation of boosters to degrade the boost-phase defense, the addition of interactive discrimination could counter this move even before it could be implemented.

A longer-term solution to the fast-burn booster problem could come from laser defensive weapons. Laser light can reach down into the atmosphere to attack even fast-burn boosters. The key requirement is to develop lasers which are powerful enough and can be retargeted quickly enough to stop the fast-burn boosters in the minute or so of their flight. Within 15 to 20 years, directed energy technology will have advanced sufficiently so that lasers may well become the primary defensive weapons. Thus, an opponent seeking to defeat a boost-phase defense by developing "fast-burn" boosters which burn out while still within the atmosphere would achieve little from this development. Lasers with effective ranges of many thousands of kilometers and retarget times of a small fraction of a second appear feasible.

Currently, the SDI organization believes that short-wave ground-based lasers of the type described earlier are the leading candidate for such laser weapons. About ten ground-based sites and up to 100 space-based relay mirrors could completely defeat a large fast-burn booster force, even if it were shielded to some degree against the lasers. An alternative, also receiving high priority by the SDI, is the space-based laser. Studies show that less than 100 long-wave infrared lasers could also defeat shielded fast-burn boosters.

Summary

The SDI is investigating both baseline defensive systems—which would meet the cost-effectiveness and survivability criteria—and responsive defense system concepts, which could defeat offensive threats specifically designed to defeat defenses. Although the United States may have to prove the feasibility of these defensive systems to the Soviet Union, it may not be necessary to actually deploy these extremely capable systems. If a cooperative transition to a defense-reliant deterrent occurs, the deployed defensive systems could be far more modest than those necessary to defeat a worst-case offensive force.

Simon P. Worden, Lieutenant Colonel in the US Air Force, is Commander, Space Defense Operations Center, and has been a Senior Research Fellow in the Institute for National Strategic Studies, National Defense University. He has also been Special Assistant to the Director/Technical Advisor to the US Delegation to the NST with the Soviet Union (Geneva), Strategic Defense Initiative Office. Lt.Col. Worden holds a B.S. degree from the University of Michigan and a Ph.D. from the University of Arizona and has been a Visiting Professor at the University of Arizona, University of California, Los Angeles, and University of Texas. He has published articles in many journals including Astrophysical Journal and contributed chapters in numerous books.

LIKELY SOVIET POLITICAL-MILITARY RESPONSES TO SDI

Sayre Stevens

Soviet Defenses: 2000-2010

This chapter attempts to anticipate the state of Soviet defenses during the 2000-2010 time-frame if the United States deploys defenses generated by the Strategic Defense Initiative (SDI).

Needless to say, one can never be certain because political initiatives and decisions, technological break-throughs, and the world environment will inevitably change beyond our predictions. Moreover, despite the heavy coverage of SDI by the Soviet press, we remain ignorant of how, precisely, they will respond to it. Longer-term responses will depend heavily upon a broad range of developments between now and the beginnings of SDI deployment.

Some Assumptions

In these circumstances, we can only make some explicit assumptions for gauging the Soviet stance toward SDI's initial deployment. The following assumptions seem reasonable:

1. Research and development in SDI has led to a US decision to start deploying an operational system in the 2000 and 2010 time period; at least some space-based Ballistic Missile Defense (BMD) components are involved. Such a decision may well be made without confidence in the ability of SDI to fulfill the more visionary goals associated with the program. In addition, the deployment decision will likely be based on the belief that the Nitze criteria—effectiveness, survivability, and defensive economic advantage at the

margin—will ultimately be met, even though they are not assured at the time of deployment. Public debate will almost surely accompany the decision to deploy SDI. Little secrecy will surround system architecture or deployment operations. In short, this deployment decision will be open and the technologies known, but the long-term efficacy of SDI will remain an open-ended question.

2. Arms control agreements do not address development of ballistic missile defenses based on other physical principles or the resolution of differing interpretations of development prohibitions in the Anti-Ballistic Missile (ABM) Treaty. Neither side will have a mutually accepted road map while changing to defense dominance. Other more hopeful scenarios are possible, but only if the United States and the Soviet Union resolve existing differences about SDI. Most importantly, I assume the Soviets will not modify the ABM Treaty to hold up early US deployment of SDI. The ABM Treaty—if not abrogated by one side or the other—will no longer effectively control the behavior of either side in preparing for BMD initiatives.

3. The Soviets will make every effort to halt, delay, or significantly constrain the SDI, but with little success. In turn, they will have simultaneously begun to explore new military technologies, systems development, and changes in force structure. Major changes in military doctrine, on the other hand, are unlikely to occur.

4. Because transition to defense dominance is occurring early, the United States will retain its strategic offensive weapons through this period.

These assumptions are not meant to portray an altogether appealing situation. Transition to a world of defensive deterrence will not be easy and is fraught with danger and uncertainty. Nevertheless, these assumptions will likely underlie deployment of SDI. I will now investigate major determinants of Soviet response to SDI and characterize them on the basis of the foregoing assumptions. Finally, I will delineate some specific responses likely to result under such a scenario.

Determinants of Soviet Response

Numerous factors are likely to shape how the Soviets will react to the SDI challenge. Traditionally, Soviet behavior is institutionalized, with senior planners doing the most policy-making. A key determinant, naturally enough, is the Soviet conception of SDI and its implications for Soviet national interests. Thus, economic considerations augment or compete with military or political imperatives. What is important is not the "correctness" of the perceptions Soviet policy makers hold, as much as how these shape their response to the problem. Abundant Soviet commentary on the Strategic Defense Initiative indicates that their perceptions now define, to a significant degree, the problem that they anticipate with SDI. Soviet policy makers and military planners alike are affected by such perceptions.

Political doctrine and foreign policy lines are particularly important. The Soviets have already undertaken a number of such initiatives, including new approaches to achieving arms control, the use of propaganda, military threats, and other foreign policy endeavors. The Soviets want to avoid the outbreak of nuclear war while exerting Soviet influence in key situations and areas throughout the world. The Strategic Defense Initiative significantly affects both tasks.

A third determinant is the guidance provided by Soviet military doctrine to balance cost and benefits against the appraised technology. The ultimate determinant is the Soviets' own evaluation of their ability to support various military, economic, technological, and weapons acquisition capabilities as they face up to the specific requirements of coping with SDI. Also involved is the question of the will to respond and the ability to sustain that will over some period of time. The degree of commitment to deal with SDI and to pay the costs associated with doing so is a function, once again, of the perception of the threat that SDI poses to the Soviet Union and its most critical objectives.

Soviet Perceptions of SDI

Political Perceptions. The Soviets seem to feel that SDI threatens important political objectives. This derives from the Soviet fear about its own international influence; its image as an unquestioned superpower. Soviet achievements to date are, and will be largely based upon, the USSR's remarkable growth achievements in military strength. The signing of the ABM Treaty and Interim Agreement of SALT I gave formal notice that the Soviets felt they had achieved a power status comparable to that of the United States. The Soviet Union attained this status through substantial economic sacrifice.

SDI, by altering the game rules of nuclear confrontation, threatens the credibility of such accomplishments. Indeed, the very purpose of SDI is to render obsolete and irrelevant those military forces which have been most significant in the growth of Soviet power. Such military accomplishments are critically important to Soviet political leadership. They represent the means for pursuing key political objectives around the world: sustaining the regime, deterring war with the "capitalist aggressors," and at the same time expanding USSR influence and dominating crises in particular situations or areas of the world.

The Soviets have demonstrated their superpower status, based principally on their military stature alone. In such circumstances, the Soviets must maintain their military strength since it reinforces their image as a superpower. SDI threatens the position of Soviet military and political leadership in varying ways. At the worst, it could lead to a form of international humiliation, something about which the Soviets are extremely sensitive and which must be considered as a real, if shadowy, consideration in dealing with Soviet responses.

Military Perceptions. Strictly military perceptions are pragmatic and directly concern their effects on the strategic balance if the Strategic Defense Initiative is pursued. Unquestionably, the Soviets now have and will continue to have, serious concerns about the reemergence of US strategic superiority based upon a combined successful SDI program and continued offensive force improvements.

Soviet concerns will almost certainly be exacerbated if the United States retains its offensive forces during early SDI deployment. If this country does not actually forego the developing and deploying of advanced offensive weapon systems, it will be hard for the Soviets to have confidence that the United States will honor its commitments to ultimately reduce offensive forces.

As noted under political perceptions, the change of ground rules embodied in SDI vastly complicates the Soviet problem. The moving target that US defensive developments presents confuses the Soviets and makes difficult the task of developing and maintaining their capacity to deal with the contingency of nuclear war. Such a stance is particularly troublesome in the Soviet system where long-range planning is the rule and relatively long lead times are necessary to change force postures and acquire new weapon systems to meet the new threat.[1] The Soviet military would much prefer to deal with an adversary whose characteristics and behavior are predictable for some time to come.

Moreover, the implications of successfully attaining SDI threaten to end the current successful Soviet approach in acquiring military forces: to lessen the technological gap while maintaining formidable forces in-being. Though the capabilities of the latter may not always adequately deal with the threat, added Soviet manpower nevertheless effectively deters the West. In Western eyes, one of the greatest appeals of SDI is its potential to leap-frog the current state of weapons development and to move to a new level of military technology making it possible to deal with the strategic confrontation in totally different ways. To accommodate such a perturbation, the Soviets must pursue the rapid incorporation of advanced technology in new weapons systems and abandon older systems which will be rendered irrelevant by new defensive developments. The Soviets will find this course a tough one to follow, and its prospect is likely to cause serious consternation among military planners and leaders.

Perceptions of SDI Technology. Soviet fear of US technology is a historic perception. The Soviets have long been concerned that US military technological development will become focused and truly energized. This consideration was surely an important factor in the Soviet decision to pursue arms control arrangements on ABMs and in concluding the ABM Treaty of 1972. Though the Soviets probably give US technological capabilities more credit than they deserve, they are conscious of their own problems in developing new technology and are substantially dissatisfied with their ability to carry science into technology and hence into specific applications.[2]

With the failure of early Soviet attempts to shut down SDI, they will face a raw technological challenge that will indeed stress their ability to translate basic scientific achievement into military hardware. The Soviets do not face this challenge with high confidence; hence, perceptions of the technological threat posed by SDI are apt to be more alarming than Westerners think.

Economic Perceptions. Economically driven perceptions are something of a mystery. Nonetheless, persuasive evidence shows that the current Soviet regime is sensitive to current economic difficulties and the constraints such difficulties impose on their ability to deal with major problems. The Soviets want to reduce military expenditures, including the allocation of skilled human resources and scarce equipment. Already indications are that the Soviet Union has, in fact, made such cuts starting with the Tenth or Eleventh Five-Year Plan.[3] Responding to SDI in a vigorous way will surely have tremendous consequences for the allocation of scarce resources in the USSR. One can only conclude that SDI must appear to Soviet economic planners as a substantial threat to needed initiatives toward economic repair. Indeed, planners see SDI as substantial as an economic, political, and military threat.

Doctrinal Imperatives

Soviet national security policy reflects two distinct doctrinal aspects: military strength and political conservatism. The Soviet military must prepare for war and establish and maintain a capability to fight and survive should war occur. Most Soviet military science and doctrine provides guidelines for conducting nuclear war. The other aspect is the political leaderships' domain which is devoted to policy intended to prevent war and to limit the threat to Soviet national security through political means.[4] In general, Soviet foreign policy has been conservative in avoiding radical moves likely to foster direct military confrontation with the West and in resisting pressures to make significant changes in the systemic premises that shape foreign policy. Soviet leaders have employed a number of tools to project an image of the USSR as committed to preserving the peace. At the same time, Soviet foreign policy has historically relied on an image of military power as a means to such political ends.

The Soviet political leadership's task in this instance is to find political means to eliminate the SDI threat. As we have seen, they perceive that threat as a serious one, particularly when viewed in political terms. The Soviet leadership must then follow a course to eliminate SDI through political initiatives, or, should that fail, to restore the foundations of power that are threatened by the United States' successful fulfillment of the initiative. But dimensions other than military appear to offer little promise. In this situation, military doctrine becomes an important factor because it guides military responses to the development of SDI.

The President's undertaking poses the possibility of a revolutionary change in current Soviet military doctrine.[5] Most importantly, it challenges the Soviet belief in the dominance of the offense in confronting the defense. Soviet doctrine is not dogmatic in taking this position, but Soviet doctrine stresses that, in the circumstances of nuclear war, the offense is likely to dominate. My earlier noted assumptions about the US deployment decision make it unlikely that the Soviets will have to abandon this element of their military doctrine by 2010. The Soviets are more apt to strengthen current offensive forces, believing that, with reliable countermeasures and accommodations to the technical military challenge of SDI, those military missions assigned to the offensive forces can still be successfully accomplished. The Soviet inclination to continue to rely upon existing military forces will slow their willingness to abandon key offensive forces, even when SDI successes make a more persuasive case for doing so. Soviet military doctrine is keyed to the early phases of a nuclear war and to disrupting the enemy's ability to function and respond during these phases. Such a mission is peculiarly suited to strategic ballistic missiles, particularly the Soviet ICBM and sea-launched ballistic missile (SLBM) forces. This doctrinal tenet is apt to strengthen further the Soviet desire to maintain ballistic missile forces and to make the accommodations necessary to ensure their ability to penetrate an SDI system.

Soviet doctrine calls for the coordinated use of forces of all kinds. Just as the United States has relied on the triad to make our strategic offensive forces richer and more robust, the Soviets rely upon the interactive use of a whole range of weapon systems to carry out the missions they have defined as critical. The Soviet doctrinal stance suggests that they will respond to SDI based upon a force structure that includes all relevant systems. Consequently, it appears unlikely that the Soviets will resort to one particular type of weapons system, but rather will spread their responses across the range of forces upon which they currently rely.

Strategic defenses will almost certainly be part of the Soviet response. Indeed, despite a doctrinal position stressing the importance of the offense, the Soviets see strategic defenses as necessary for successfully waging nuclear war. The Soviets, through their sustained investment in strategic defensive forces, have demonstrated a belief in their importance.

In developing strategic defenses as well as other forces, the Soviets have shown a readiness to accept the importance of even partially limiting damage to the Soviet Union if nuclear war occurs. Since the control of military doctrine has traditionally rested with the military services, the services have been successful in establishing their military requirements for new and improved weapons systems.

With the coordinated use of forces of all kinds comes a Soviet realization that individual weapons systems can also be coordinated to limit the disruptive damage of a nuclear attack. Thus, the Soviets have relied on active defenses to protect against aerodynamic threats; they have deployed an ABM system to defend against limited ballistic missile attack; they have maintained passive defenses, not only to protect selected segments of the population, but also to undertake counterforce strikes against US strategic nuclear weapons as well. Damage limitation—that is the readiness to invest in weapons systems able to contribute significantly, if not entirely satisfactorily, to limit damage in a nuclear war—will likely be an important attribute of the overall Soviet response to SDI.

Again, the tenets of Soviet military doctrine will not change because of the United States' early deployment of SDI mission elements.[6] The Soviets have long resisted such basic change. Soviet military planners will continue to stress traditional military doctrine: time-urgent attacks on command, control, communications and intelligence (C³I) and other nuclear forces; measures to ensure the survivability of their own forces; strategic defenses critical to limiting damage resulting from a US nuclear attack; and maintaining forces for peripheral attack and conventional theater warfare.

Soviet Ability to Respond

Given all of these formulations of the SDI problem which result from Soviet perceptions and predilections as to how they should respond to the challenge, how will the Soviets actually respond?

Political Opportunities. Though the Soviets will have failed to halt or significantly slow SDI if first deployment occurs in the 2000-2010 time-frame, they can constrain it to more acceptable levels and delay the process of system deployment. Continued arms control imperatives are likely to have wide appeal throughout this period and will become particularly important during actual deployment.

One question leaps out from the foregoing assumptions: given the inability of the United States and the Soviet Union to resolve their differences about SDI, what has become of arms control? The Soviets continue to believe that broadly based expectations about arms control will succeed in reducing military tensions and the likelihood of war. The Soviets continually contend that arms control agreements are by themselves key to the preservation of peace.[7] Indeed, this line has had strong appeal in the West. Some credible arms control effort is necessary to maintain the support of US allies and the Congress. Pressures for reestablishing mutually agreed constraints on military forces will continue to come from domestic populations and organizations as well as other states and international organizations.

Should existing agreements effectively fail (as assumed here), however, a new start may be necessary. This situation poses a substantially more difficult problem than merely extending or elaborating established agreements. Current arms negotiations depend mainly on confrontational strategies between the two countries.[8] A return to more active and less competitive relationships may be fostered by the arms control impasse and the political need to temper the confrontation on military matters. Whatever the case, mutual participation in arms control exploration will almost surely continue. The two countries will undoubtedly seek new approaches to avoid the intractable issues of earlier negotiations. Should they fail to show appropriate initiative in such efforts, international organizations are likely to play a much larger multilateral role.

The Soviets have traditionally been effective in manipulating the desires and the pressures for arms control agreements and in pursuing objectives through arms control that are important to Soviet objectives. The Soviets will continue such a policy during the US deployment decision and the first steps toward deployment.

Economic Constraints. Despite apparent Soviet desires to reduce or at least contain their military expenditures, it is very difficult to identify specific economic measures concerning their response to SDI. Real economic problems continue and the pressures to reduce military resources are strong, but the Soviets will respond to an SDI threat they believe is serious. One can only conclude that the Soviets will do what they have done in the past: spend money and allocate scarce resources to counter the SDI threat. As in the past, funds will be diverted from other investments and economic sectors. We simply cannot rely on the idea that SDI will force the Soviets into actions they are economically incapable of performing.

Technology Development. We have already noted Soviet difficulties in meeting the technological challenges associated with SDI. Efforts are underway to improve the application of advanced technology to weapons systems. On the one hand, the defense technology of the Soviet Union is a model for other parts of the Soviet economy to emulate. On the other hand, however, Soviet economists are dissatisfied with the exploitation of research and development (R&D) and its introduction into the weapons acquisition process.

In general, the Soviet Union follows an acquisition policy that limits technological risk to every possible extent. More adventurous approaches have proven to be slow, but periodic advancements improve the follow-on systems. Ultimately, weapons systems of real effectiveness result from this process. Still, success in countering or emulating SDI poses a serious technological challenge to the Soviet Union. Although a number of organizational and procedural fixes have been tried in the past, now new steps are being taken to improve the research and development process. Even so, the Soviets are not likely to make significant improvements in the next 10 years.[9]

Technology transfer has eased this problem because the Soviets have been able to follow up on Western advances in a number of areas through the systematic acquisition and exploitation of foreign technology. Such stealing of technology cannot replace entirely the formidable scientific work that the Soviets are conducting in working weapons systems. This situation suggests that the USSR may follow the United States' lead in SDI, but at some distance in time. Although early technological accomplishments may lag behind those of the United States, the Soviets will pursue the problem with persistence and gradually introduce a system that may well become a significant factor in the strategic balance.

Insofar as the development of countermeasures is concerned, the needed technology is certainly within reach of Soviet scientists and engineers. In the 2000-2010 time period, the Soviets will first display their ability to carry through most of the technical countermeasure work to deal with SDI as we now perceive it.

Weapons Acquisition Capabilities. The Soviets have strong momentum to design, develop, and produce advanced weapons systems. The USSR has invested in the capability to develop and produce such weapons, and has seen that grow since the early 1960s.

As already noted, Soviet weapons acquisition capability is characterized by a low risk approach toward incorporating advanced technology. The planning cycle centers on the Soviet five-year plans which are rigid, hierarchical, and depend on interaction among customers, developers, producers, suppliers, and other intrastructural elements. While the planning process tends to be sticky and resists change, a persistent program of force extension and enhancement makes up for these shortcomings. Once established, the Soviet acquisition process runs in a steady, even relentless fashion. While peculiarities in the Soviet acquisition process cause disadvantages in rapidly fielding high technology responses to SDI, they give the Soviet Union significant advantages to pursue countermeasures to it.

The Will to Respond. Soviet perceptions of the American program force the Soviets to react vigorously and with concentration toward SDI. The Soviet leadership can develop, nurture, and sustain a broad-based will among its people. This Soviet endeavor mirrors the Reagan Administration's effort to give SDI a high profile, so as to capture the American public's imagination and enthusiasm. Early indicators suggest Soviet SDI propaganda has generated among its own people a popular view of US behavior as provocative, threatening, and incompatible with Soviet interests. Clearly, the Soviets are pursuing a program that will counter SDI even though such a program may be costly and unpopular to

Soviet citizens. If the United States deploys SDI, Soviet citizens will vilify the United States and SDI. The Soviet leadership will cultivate such a feeling no matter what the cost.

Some Specific Responses

Let us now consider what all these factors mean in terms of specific Soviet responses if the United States should, after the year 2000, deploy the first operational elements of an SDI system. A formidable set of coordinated Soviet military forces now exists to respond militarily. However, this force structure is not very flexible, will be difficult to change rapidly and radically, and will have created its own institutional imperatives to responding fully to SDI. The bottom line is that it will not be easy for the Soviets to make substantial changes quickly to counter initial SDI development. Nevertheless, the Soviets will make some changes during the intervening time period, particularly if political efforts to halt or slow the program fail.

A single, grand counter to SDI is not likely to make up the entire Soviet response because it would lack the reliability and certainty that the Soviets traditionally seek. Instead, the Soviets will likely turn to a full range of responses to the US SDI program. Moreover, until more specific features of the ultimate SDI system are defined and disclosed, it will be difficult to predict precise Soviet countermeasures. As a result, moderate Soviet responses employing gradual modifications of the current force structure are more likely.

International Ballistic Missiles (ICBMs). Land-based ICBMs have long constituted the heart of Soviet strategic offensive forces. Soviets have proliferated and improved these weapons systems and are now introducing the fifth generation of such weapons. They have progressed from a very uncertain and cumbersome SS-6 to advanced mobile systems which could well reach US hard targets while maintaining a substantial degree of survivability themselves. It will be extraordinarily difficult for the Soviets to abandon these weapons systems.

As noted above, Soviet doctrine gives high value to such systems in the early phases of war when the counterforce mission is particularly important and the payoffs, associated with disrupting the enemy's ability to manage his forces and to respond, are very high. These time-urgent missions are particularly well-suited to Soviet ICBM doctrine.

Overwhelming an early SDI system with offensive missile forces will offer an attractive approach for some time, and Soviet uncertainties about SDI will suggest it to be a prudent course to follow, particularly if the United States maintains its own offensive missile forces. As a first counter to an emerging SDI system, the appeal of increasing numbers of Soviet ICBMs will be strong. Thus, it is likely that during our first deployment of SDI elements, we will be facing more rather than fewer ICBMs. It is likely, too, that Soviet ICBMs will be increasingly mobile because of growing US hard target capabilities and Soviet concern about our combined SDI and substantially improved offensive capabilities.

The requirement for a penetrating counterforce capability leads one to expect more MIRV'd SS-24s, but the rail-basing characteristics of that system limits how many can be deployed in mobile fashion. Thus, we must also expect to see more improved SS-25s in the Soviet force. We may in fact see not only these specific systems but, in addition, follow-on systems with substantial improvements that will strengthen their ability to fulfill assigned missions. Finally, currently deployed systems, such as the SS-18 and SS-19, will be further improved or replaced with new missile systems, and they will continue to contribute to the total Soviet force.[10]

If the Soviets are going to pursue this ICBM strategy, they must also take the steps to add countermeasures to ICBMs that will enable them to penetrate the emerging SDI system. This task will be made difficult because SDI still lacks an early definition. Fine tuning architectural design and choosing of sensor systems will not be possible much before 2000. Thus, Soviets must use broad experimentation and general approaches to develop countermeasures.

Specific activities will occur as more is learned about the actual structure of the SDI system and the technologies chosen to implement it. The Soviets will work hard at collecting this information and will, by the time deployment begins, have amassed considerable information about the program, its design characteristics, and where it is leading. The United States will certainly provide protection for the true secrets bearing on SDI. Still, the Soviets are likely to have some success in penetrating the security structure and collecting information about the system, which we will be trying to protect.

When deployment begins, Soviet countermeasure investigation should be in full bloom. The direction of the US program, its architecture and its initial technological dependencies, should be well-established and ready for promising countermeasures. We will likely be unable to distinguish those countermeasures (test flights, and others) which will be implemented in the Soviet forces and those which will never get beyond the investigative stages. Thus, we will be left with the problem of somehow having to deal with most of them.

Soviet investigation of some specific countermeasures can be expected, though, while it is easy to list a number, it is very difficult to deal with such considerations as virtual attrition. Soviet development of ICBM propulsion systems with shorter burn times, not necessarily fast burn times, would greatly complicate the problem of boost-phase intercept and is in keeping with the cautious Soviet approach of incorporating new technology and transitioning to solid propellant systems. The Soviets will likely complicate booster signatures that might be detected by the sensor elements of a SDI boost-phase intercept system to identify targets and provide guidance to kinetic energy weapons. Booster decoys are also a possibility: older, stored, and not deployed missiles that are in the inventory, as well as propulsion stages with dummy payloads that might be produced in large numbers.

To cope with the problem of midcourse intercept, the Soviets will likely shorten the propulsion times of busses for the deployment of multiple independently targetable reentry vehicles (MIRVs) to reduce their vulnerability. Once reenty vehicle (RV) deployment has occurred, the Soviets will have to modify the signature of the RVs so that they will be difficult to discriminate from decoys. Decoys must be developed that will overwhelm the abilities of the SDI system to cope with midcourse intercept as well as to complicate the problems of terminal defense. Maneuverable reentry vehicles, which the Soviets have investigated, are also likely to be a part of this arsenal of countermeasures.

More dramatic approaches are also a possibility. The Soviets might, for example, return to their earlier fractional orbital bombardment system (FOBS) to confound a defensive system unprepared for such an attack. Other countermeasure possibilities exist and, indeed, the Soviets will investigate all of them. But, in the early phase of SDI, the list provided here indicates the dimensions of the countermeasure development problem faced by the Soviets and of the countermeasure problem posed to the United States.

Submarine-Launched Ballistic Missiles (SLBMs). The Soviets will almost certainly retain their commitment to submarine-launched ballistic missiles, along with follow-on systems to those currently deployed.[11] The number of weapons carried by these missiles has grown significantly in recent years, and we can expect improved systems to appear in the future. Some modifications for SDI appear to be attractive. In fact, the Soviets seem convinced of the advantage of using depressed trajectories by ballistic missile submarines relatively close to our coastline. Such a Soviet ploy is very promising because of the limited amount of time it allows for decisionmaking and the shortened period of SLBM vulnerability to defensive action. We can also expect reentry vehicle modifications and the development of countermeasures, many of which will match those developed for ICBMs. In short, submarine-launched ballistic missiles will be a significant part of the Soviet force and will require accommodations once SDI is deployed.

Cruise Missiles. The Soviets have an energetic program of cruise missile development underway and will need little urging to employ cruise missiles to cover a larger number of strategic missions.[12] The Soviet cruise missile program represents the newest stage in the steady and gradual improvement of a particular class of weapons system over the course of many years. Older Soviet cruise systems were large and, for the most part, employed earlier aircraft engine technology. Newer systems are small, based upon the bypass jet engine, and are being developed in air-, sea-, and ground-launched modes. Though an SDI counter to the cruise missile threat is promised, the program has not yet focused on it; in addition, the absence of conventional air defenses in the United States argues for an increased Soviet investment in cruise missiles.

More cruise missiles will likely enter the Soviet arsenal during the period of concern. Whether or not this increase will accompany increases in Soviet strategic bombers is unclear. The Blackjack bomber will probably emerge as a cruise missile carrier for the new AS-15 air-launched cruise missile (ALCM), the first of the new cruise missiles now under development and likely to become operational.[13] Quite possibly a Soviet technology push will produce a penetrating bomber employing low observable technology and carrying advanced air-to-surface missiles by the year 2000.

Peripheral Attack. Peripheral attack forces will surely continue to receive much attention, particularly those forces committed to confronting NATO. Some improvements are likely in response to promised SDI NATO defense, but may emerge sooner than expected because of present NATO discussions about the developing Anti-Tactical Missile (ATM) systems to deal with the SS-20. Despite such talk, it is very likely that mobile intermediate range ballistic missiles (IRBMs)—the SS-20s—will be retained, improved, and replaced with newer systems by the year 2000. Cruise missiles also will be key elements in the weapons arsenal for peripheral attack. As with strategic offensive weapons, the use of depressed trajectories for submarine-launched ballistic missiles against NATO is also a possibility.

This paper consciously omits the general purpose forces used for conventional theater warfare and the priority the Soviets give to their maintenance and improvement. An SDI system may leave them largely unaffected. On the other hand, Soviet belief that SDI might make strategic nuclear offenses untenable could unchain Soviet conventional force, an expressed concern of our European allies. An intriguing twist accompanies this easy characterization of the situation. The Soviets have railed repeatedly against the "space-strike weapons" embodied in SDI, suggesting that they will pose a threat to targets on the ground. If these worries are real and not just propaganda, the Soviets will have to accommodate their concern for ground force survival with the SDI threat. In any event, I will leave treatment of this subject to other analysts.

Strategic Defenses. Despite the doctrinal priority given to offensive weapons systems in an era of strategic nuclear war, the Soviets have made a formidable commitment to develop strategic defenses. After World War II, Soviet planners developed air defenses that would provide protection against mass bomber raids. From that beginning, the Soviets have institutionalized a strategic defense establishment that has investigated, developed, and deployed weapons systems able to counter increasingly advanced aerodynamic threats. The Soviets have developed and deployed ballistic missile defenses, and they have started to deal with threats posed by space-based vehicles. This history of Soviet commitment to strategic defenses should make the new-found enthusiasm of the United States for such weapons systems appear qualified.[14]

Since the signing of the ABM Treaty, the Soviets have maintained a steady R&D program of new ballistic missile defenses within the constraints of the treaty. Because of Soviet readiness to carry out activities at the limits of treaty provisions, the USSR has avoided the stultifying ballistic missile defense R&D activities that have occurred in the United States.

Soviet R&D activities have succeeded so well since the ABM Treaty that their ABM-X-3 system now appears available for widespread deployment. The Moscow ABM system, which became operational shortly after the signing of the ABM Treaty, is now being modified and improved, but will have limited capability. Improvements underway are establishing a base for a substantially larger defense of the Moscow region, even in the absence of ABM Treaty constraints. Regarding conventional BMD development, the Soviets appear poised for a substantially broader deployment of defenses.

Still, they may not be ready to take such a step. Indeed, the SDI initiative and the Soviet perception of this threat appears to make them more stalwart champions of preserving the treaty and gaining its protection. Should erosion of the treaty continue, however, the Soviets may likely capitalize on their advantage to put systems into the field much more quickly than the United States. Such Soviet deployment would probably first involve strengthening the Moscow defense and deploying interceptors in larger numbers than currently allowed by the treaty; they would then deploy systems to protect military and industrial centers in the western USSR. Ultimately, the Soviets could establish a nationwide system of terminal defenses well before assumed US initial deployment of SDI, as considered in this paper.

This work on more conventional BMD systems has included investigation of weapons "based on other physical principles."[15] Both ground-based and space-based weapons seem to be under investigation. The new physical principles involved include laser and particle beam weapons systems, advanced kinetic energy weapons, as well as weapons using radio frequencies at high power as the kill mechanism. In addition, substantial work is underway on developing space systems suitable for robust orbital operations. In short, the Soviets have been continuously conducting a low-profile investigation of the technologies required to move their own strategic defenses to new levels of capability and effectiveness.

Most likely this program represents the major Soviet response to the US decision to pursue the Strategic Defense Initiative. Prior to this time, the Soviet program has been debated and probably viewed as an uncertain undertaking. The United States contributes to this effort, and the result is likely to mean greater funding, commitment, and acceptance by the Soviet leadership. In any event, the Soviets will find it difficult to accept a patronizing US offer to make available the technology developed here so the Soviets, too, can enjoy the benefits of defense dominance. The Soviets will not rely upon our readiness to make that technology transfer once we have established this new approach to strategic defense. Their perception that SDI is a strategy for achieving unmatched first-strike capability, combined with offensive weapons system improvements, leaves them skeptical about the credibility of such an offer.

For these reasons, we can expect that the Soviet advanced technology program will accelerate and will represent Soviet attempts to achieve many of the goals we are pursuing in the United States. Technology demonstrations will likely occur in the Soviet program later this century and into the next, which will put actual hardware into space with observable characteristics and performance significant to the SDI mission. Observers may well interpret these demonstrations as prototype SDI elements and characterize them in terms of US design goals. Thus, we will conclude that the Soviet program is in close competition with that of the United States.

Early Soviet efforts, however, will be much more limited in scope than ours, and what appear to be prototype elements of the system may indeed be merely technology demonstrations. This sort of apparent Soviet breakthrough has occurred many times in the past as early Soviet systems have been put into the field or orbit without ever rapidly developing into full-blown systems. Still, Soviet persistence usually yields operational systems that gradually develop significant capabilities as they are improved and replaced with newer versions.

The Soviets enjoy some significant advantages over the United States in undertaking an SDI-like program. Their doctrine of damage limitation allows them to develop and deploy elements that are more easily achievable, and to justify those developments which contribute to the workings of a much larger coordinated system. The Soviets are optimistic and have an acquisition system in place that ensures such improvements. Follow-on systems will occur. SDI involves numerous distant goals, and successful fulfillment of the program requires long-range, steady commitment. The Soviets have demonstrated a better ability to pursue long-term and uncertain goals than has the United States. Because of their ability to sustain momentum, the Soviets are more likely to maintain program viability in circumstances which might lead to its abandonment in the United States. A worrisome possibility is that at the end of the SDI adventure—long after the time period of concern here—the Soviets alone may possess deployed SDI defenses while the United States may have abandoned its effort. If so, the resultant asymmetrical strategic defenses will radically affect the strategic balance and have extremely destabilizing effects.

Current Soviet strategic defenses include anti-satellite (ASAT) capabilities, but they offer little promise of effectively countering SDI.[16] If the Soviets do use anti-satellite defenses to counter an SDI deployment, they must develop a substantially different type of system than their current orbital interceptor. Indeed, large numbers of small, widely deployed interceptors will be required. Because serious questions about the survivability of SDI exist, the Soviets will seriously investigate ways to attack such a defense. If they develop appropriate anti-satellite weapons, they will look for attack scenarios to neutralize selected system elements, such as battle management and C³I platforms and selected sensor elements that will cripple the use of the overall system. Such efforts, however, await full SDI system definition and can only take place substantially later in program development. In addition, the Soviets will undoubtedly explore larger yield detonations in space to produce environments incompatible to an SDI system. However, an inability to test such weapons in space will make it difficult for the Soviets to evaluate such tactics.

The question has frequently been raised whether or not the Soviets might launch an attack during the deployment of an SDI system. A substantial advantage exists for mounting such an attack before sufficient elements of SDI are in place to defend against an anti-satellite attack. Despite such advantages, however, the Soviets will likely doubt the effectiveness of the SDI system, and be so unsure of their ability to cope with it, that they would not turn to so provocative an action. More likely they will choose to degrade the system through ground-based laser weapons capable of achieving substantial attrition.

Most importantly Soviet strategic defenses include key additional elements that will accompany any fully developed SDI system, including air defenses and passive defenses to protect the leadership, military forces, selected elements of the population, and key installations in case of a nuclear attack. As noted above, air defenses have traditionally been a major concern in the

Soviet Union, and the Soviets have been relentless in extending and improving them.[17] New systems are now under development, while older systems are being enhanced or replaced to meet improvements in the offensive aerodynamic threat. In sum, one can say that the foundations on which to build a full and effective system of strategic defenses are far, far better established in the Soviet Union than in the United States.

Finally, we must consider some specific political moves that the Soviets might make, should the United States decide to deploy SDI defenses in 2000. The Soviets will continue to slow or constrain the US effort and will take whatever advantage they can of any US culpability for eroding or breaking the ABM Treaty as a result of its SDI efforts. They will surely endeavor to exploit disagreements among the NATO allies about that deployment decision. At this early stage our NATO partners probably do not sense the same advantages as the United States since the defense SDI can provide to Europe will be significantly less than that to the United States. Thus, the Soviets will make every effort to nurture fears that the United States has decoupled its own defense from that of Europe. They will continue to deride the effectiveness, cost, and provocative nature of the SDI system.

We must be prepared to face a likely Soviet ultimatum of some magnitude on the deployment of "space strike weapons" or other provocative elements of the SDI system. Certainly, the Soviets will make some last-ditch efforts to stop deployment, perhaps by accusing the United States of making the ultimate provocative move in its confrontation with the Soviet Union and with the progressive world as a whole.

Thus, a vision of the world of 2000-2010 emerges where both the United States and the Soviet Union are actively engaged in significant upgrading of both offensive and defensive weapons systems. With the Soviet Union, the full range of force elements is involved, with emphasis on constant improvements of all systems. Many of the pessimistic characterizations of this period could well have more satisfying alternatives, but the current course seems headed in the direction outlined here. Unless a significant change occurs, increased technological tension will be the order of the day. Such an outcome is not inevitable, but unless we change current trends, we have little reason to expect a different outcome.

Sayre Stevens is executive vice president of the System Planning Corporation and a member of the Defense Science Board. For over 21 years he served in the Central Intelligence Agency in a variety of positions involving technical intelligence analysis and intelligence-related research and development. He served as advisor on the US SALT I delegation. As Deputy Director for Intelligence he was responsible for all the CIA's intelligence analysis. Dr. Stevens holds a Ph.D. degree from the University of Washington and has contributed articles to many books and journals.

NOTES

1. Much has been written on this characteristic of the Soviet weapons acquisition process. See, for example, Arthur J. Alexander, *Decision Making in Soviet Weapons Procurement* (London: IISS, Adelphi Papers Number 147 and 148, 1978), pp. 25-27.

2. Gorbachev, in particular, has emphasized the need to accelerate scientific and technical progress. See, *A Study of Soviet Science* (December 1985). This study was based, in part, on interviews with 100 US scientists with Soviet associations. It was distributed by George A. Keyworth, Science Advisor to the President.

3. Robert W. Campbell, "Discussion Paper on Economy, Society, and Security," in Dick Clark, *United States-Soviet Relations: Building A Consensus Policy* (Aspen Institute for Humanistic Studies, 1985), pp. 14-15.

4. See David Holloway, *The Soviet Union and the Arms Race* (New Haven, CT: Yale University Press, 1983), pp. 29-58; and Edward L. Warner III, "Key Issues in Contemporary Soviet Military Policy," in Clark, *US-Soviet Relations*, pp. 41-43.

5. Much has been written on Soviet military doctrine. For its particular relationship to BMD, see Sidney Graybeal and Daniel Goure, "Soviet Ballistic Missile Defense (BMD) Objectives: Past, Present, and Future," in Ballistic Missile Defense Advanced Technology Center, *US Arms Control Objectives and the Implications for Ballistic Missile Defense* (Cambridge, MA: Puritan Press, 1980), pp. 69-90.

6. Warner, "Soviet Military Policy," p. 44.

7. Adam Ulam, "Soviet Foreign Policy," in Clark, *US-Soviet Relations*, p. 26.

8. See William G. Hyland, "United States-Soviet Relations," in Clark, *US-Soviet Relations*, pp. 5-9.

9. *A Study of Soviet Science*, pp. 10-13; 18-20.

10. For information on the Soviet ICBM force see, *Soviet Military Power, 1986* (Washington, DC: Government Printing Office, 1986), pp. 23-28.

11. Ibid., pp. 28-31.

12. Ibid., pp. 33-34.

13. Ibid., pp. 31-33.

14. See my "The Soviet BMD Program," in Ashton B. Carter and David Schwartz (eds.), *Ballistic Missile Defense* (Washington, DC: The Brookings Institution, 1984), pp. 182-220, for an overview of Soviet strategic defensive developments.

15. *Soviet Military Power, 1986*, pp. 45-48.

16. Ibid., pp. 48-51 and *Soviet Strategic Defense Programs* (Washington, DC: Department of Defense, October 1985). See also Alexander, *Soviet Weapons Procurement,* pp. 37-39 for a discussion of the origins of these programs.

17. Ibid., pp. 53-57.

THE IMPACT OF SDI ON US-SOVIET RELATIONS

Paul H. Nitze

In addressing the impact of SDI on US-Soviet relations, I would like to focus primarily on the near term, the period extending into the early 1990s during which the SDI research program seeks to answer the questions President Reagan posed. These center on the feasibility of a militarily effective, survivable, and cost-effective strategic defense. This period will be critical for our scientists and engineers who must overcome daunting technical challenges; for our politicians who must find the resources and political measures to undergird these efforts; and for our diplomats and negotiators who must seek to convince the Soviet leadership that strategic defenses can serve the mutual interests of the United States and the Soviet Union. It is this latter task which I will explore, the likely political impact of our SDI research efforts on the Soviet leadership.

Our understanding of what happens behind the Kremlin walls has advanced beyond where it was half a century ago when Winston Churchill described Russia as "a riddle, wrapped in a mystery, inside an enigma." We have gotten glimpses from classified sources and from public memoirs such as *Khrushchev Remembers*. It would be misleading, however, to imply that such glimpses enable us to predict Soviet tactical behavior with high confidence, although we can have a pretty good idea of the Soviets' overall strategic approach.

The modest level of confidence we do have in predicting Soviet behavior must be further qualified by the Soviet capacity for surprise and sudden reversals of policy. The Soviet capacity for surprise is inherently greater than that of the West, where there is little or no tolerance for adopting patently inequitable positions, even in the context of negotiating tactics. Western governments must strive to keep their publics informed and must consider likely public reactions to any sudden change in policy. Moreover, few internal US governmental policy deliberations remain invisible to readers of the American press. In stark contrast to the situation in the West, the Soviets tend to conduct policy deliberations in complete secrecy, begin negotiations with totally one-sided positions, and on occasion reverse policy positions with dazzling speed.

What the Soviets Have Said

Analysis should therefore begin with a review of available evidence rather than with fixed notions of how the Soviets will react to the US SDI program. Such a review should incorporate what the Soviets have said and what they have actually done. Five themes emerge from recent Soviet commentary on SDI:

1. *That the SDI program represents an effort by the US to gain strategic superiority over the Soviet Union by acquiring a first-strike capability.* The Soviets charge that SDI is intended to lead to a first-strike capability in two ways, one indirectly and the other directly. Effective strategic defenses deployed over the United States would allow it to launch a first strike attack against the Soviet Union without fear of the retaliation which would follow. Development of SDI technologies would also provide the United States with an opportunity to deploy space-based systems designed to attack targets on the ground, at sea, and in the air.

2. *That the Soviets seek "to prevent an arms race in space."* The Soviets pressed this formulation at the January 1985 meeting between then-Foreign Minister Gromyko and Secretary Shultz, and sought to reiterate it in the Joint Statement following the November 1985 Summit between General Secretary Gorbachev and President Reagan. The Soviets contend that the SDI program will inevitably lead to an unconstrained arms competition in a realm heretofore free of such competition. Indeed, the Soviets assert that space, which they imply

is not yet "militarized," should be kept free of military missions and forces. The Soviets label the unwillingness of the United States to end the SDI research program as an American breach of the commitments undertaken "to prevent an arms race in space."

3. *That in order to prevent an arms race in space, the Soviets seek a ban on the research, development, testing, and deployment of "space-strike arms."* The Soviets originally defined "space-strike arms" as weapons based in space which are designed to attack targets in space and on earth, and weapons on earth which are designed to attack objects in space. In Geneva they have modified this assertion to cover satellites in space, rather than objects in space. This Soviet position implies a spectrum of constraints that goes far beyond the limits of the 1967 Outer Space Treaty and the 1972 ABM Treaty, to include a ban on all space-based antiballistic missiles, all space-based ground attack weapons, and all anti-satellite weapons of any basing mode. However, the Soviet definition of "space-strike arms" excludes an important area of existing Soviet advantage—ground-based ABM systems—which are capable of attacking satellites or ballistic missile warheads in space. Moreover, the Soviet-proposed ban on "scientific research" on what they call "space-strike arms" also uses the criterion of intention rather than capability. Therefore, the Soviet proposal would ban US SDI research because its purpose (to defend against nuclear weapons) is known, but leave similar Soviet research untouched (because the Soviets deny that their equivalent research has a military purpose).

4. *That if the United States does not agree to a ban on "space-strike arms," there can be no agreement limiting strategic offensive arms.* The Soviets express full confidence in being able to take the necessary counter-measures to SDI, and suggest that proliferation of Soviet offensive systems would be one of the means required to do so. Thus, they will not accept reductions or even limits on offensive systems if the United States refuses

limits on "space-strike arms," beyond these already agreed to under the ABM Treaty.

5. *That involvement in the US SDI program by third countries will necessarily damage the bilateral relationships between those countries and the Soviet Union.* As an extension of their claim that the SDI program is a US attempt to gain military superiority over the Soviet Union, the Soviets assert that any collusion in that effort by other countries must be regarded as an unfriendly act which will have negative consequences for those countries' bilateral relations with the Soviet Union.

Taken at face value, these themes portray an ominous prospect for the impact of SDI on US-Soviet relations, and indeed on global stability. SDI would not only prohibit any movement away from deterrence based on the threat of nuclear retaliation; it would also make impossible mutual and stabilizing reductions in strategic offensive weaponry which could significantly improve our existing system of deterrence. Some analysts stop at this point, assert that the negative impact of SDI is obvious, and conclude that the United States must therefore abandon SDI before it is too late.

However, Soviet doctrine reflects constant pursuit of military advantages in both offensive and defensive forces, and preserving current advantages in both areas. Soviet assertions about SDI must be considered with these objectives in mind. To conclude otherwise ignores obvious Soviet incentives for encouraging Western publics to accept these alleged Soviet perceptions, even if actual Soviet concerns are quite different. The Soviets seek to portray the United States as a nation seeking unilateral advantage, and thereby fueling the arms race. The Soviets' continually imply that support for SDI research will make arms control agreements impossible and improvements in bilateral relationships with the Soviet Union unlikely. Thus, to understand the impact of SDI on US-Soviet relations, we must go beyond Soviet public statements and examine what the Soviet Union has actually done:

What the Soviets Have Done

1. *They have stressed the importance of strategic defense.* For Western observers, one of the most striking features of the Soviet military defense establishment and its guiding doctrines is the emphasis placed on strategic defense. In the post-war era, the Soviet Union has devoted approximately the same level of resources to strategic defense as it has to its massive buildup of strategic offensive forces. Heavy Soviet investments in strategic defenses have continued even at a time when the United States was de-emphasizing strategic defenses because we no longer perceived them to be cost-effective.

• While the United States elected not to maintain the 100 ABM missile interceptors allowed under the 1972 ABM Treaty and subsequent protocol, the Soviets both deployed and modernized such systems.

• While the United States maintained a modest ballistic missile defense research and development effort, the Soviets undertook an ambitious research and development effort to improve both existing fixed ground-based systems and to explore exotic new technologies.

• While the United States for all intents and purposes abandoned the goal of providing an effective air defense of the country in the mid-1960s, the Soviet Union has maintained and modernized the world's largest strategic air defense system.

• While the United States has scrupulously adhered to the ABM Treaty, the Soviets have violated an important provision of that treaty and have undertaken activities that suggest they may be preparing an ABM defense of their national territory.

Thus no evidence exists concerning Soviet reticence about the concept of strategic defense.

2. *They have pursued military uses of space.* The Soviets have never manifested a genuine concern about

keeping space free of military systems. Instead, they have always maintained a keen interest in exploiting space for military purposes. For example, the Soviet space program has always had a major military component. The majority of military satellites orbiting in space today belong to the Soviet Union, and the majority of their space launches are military missions.

The Soviet Union was the first nation to develop and deploy intercontinental ballistic missiles which launch nuclear warheads on a ballistic trajectory transversing space. The Soviet Union was the only nation ever to develop and deploy a fractional orbital bombardment system (FOBS)—which has since been outlawed—capable of attacking ground targets in the United States with nuclear weapons from space orbit. The Soviets have now the world's only operational anti-satellite (ASAT) system, and they have also an operational anti-ballistic missile (ABM) system based around Moscow designed to destroy ballistic missile reentry vehicles in space with nuclear warheads. (These latter three weapons systems, FOBS, ASAT, and ABM, would fit squarely into the Soviet definition of "space-strike arms," if that definition were based upon capabilities rather than the subjectively determined intent of the designers.) Similarly, the Soviets assert that our SDI research, and not their comparable research, is designed to create "space-strike arms."

I recite these points not to suggest that the Soviets are using space in contravention of existing arms control agreements, nor to imply that they alone stress the military uses of space, some of which are vital for security and for international stability. Rather, I mention these points to explain why the United States cannot take seriously the Soviet charge that SDI would result in the "militarization of space." The Soviet public line is designed to obfuscate Soviet capabilities and intentions with regard to the uses of space, and detracts from constructive dialogue on defense and space issues in Geneva.

The United States has agreed to the announced Soviet goal of "preventing an arms race in space." The United States could accept this Soviet proposal because the SDI concept we are pursuing is in fact the *opposite* of an "arms race." SDI envisions a jointly managed approach designed to maintain proper control, at all times, over the mix of offensive and defensive systems of both sides, thereby increasing the confidence of all nations in the stability of the evolving strategic balance. We are seeking, even now, to discuss with the Soviets in Geneva how a transition to a stabilizing and more defense-reliant strategic regime could occur, should effective defenses prove feasible.

3. *They have resumed arms control talks.* We can gain some perspective by recalling what has happened since the President announced the Strategic Defense Initiative in March of 1983. Following the initial deployments of US longer-range intermediate nuclear force (LRINF) missiles in Europe toward the end of 1983, the Soviets walked out of both the INF and Strategic Arms Talks (START) negotiations in Geneva. Soviet negotiators said at the time that it would not be possible to resume these negotiations until the United States withdrew its longer-range intermediate nuclear force missiles from Europe. During 1984 and the beginning of fiscal year 1985, the President's articulation of a new initiative in strategic defense was translated into an integrated program with significantly enhanced funding over previous levels. US LRINF deployments, meanwhile, continued on schedule. In January 1985, the Soviet Union agreed to resume the START and INF negotiations, coupled with new negotiations on defense and space arms.

It would be oversimplified, I believe, to assert that SDI alone brought the Soviets back to the negotiating table. Other important reasons influenced the Soviets to resume the talks. However, it would be reasonable to conclude that SDI alone played a significant part in getting the Soviets to return to negotiations.

4. They have somewhat narrowed their differences at negotiations. Significant boulders continue to block the path of progress at the negotiations on nuclear and space arms which began at Geneva in March 1985. Nonetheless, some positive movement has taken place. The Soviet counter-proposal in September/October 1985 to our opening position and the US response in November narrowed the differences between the two sides on some important issues. The joint statement between President Reagan and General Secretary Gorbachev at the November summit called for early progress in the negotiations, building on areas of common ground, particularly "the principle of 50 percent reductions in the nuclear arms of the United States and USSR appropriately applied," and "the idea of an interim INF agreement." Mr. Gorbachev's proposal of January 15, 1986 showed a willingness for some compromise in the Soviet position on INF. While the Soviets still demanded unacceptable actions from third parties as preconditions to an agreement, the Soviets have dropped their claim for direct numerical compensation for British and French forces. However, in the last round of the negotiations, the Soviets again resorted to abstractions and generalities. Nonetheless, potential for convergence of views exists in future rounds on several issues, including reductions in LRINF missiles, ICBM warheads, total ballistic missile warheads, ballistic missile throw-weight, and in the total numbers of ballistic missiles and heavy bombers.

The United States' vigorous pursuit of SDI research during the negotiations has not prevented us from developing some important areas of potential common ground. Some observers assert that SDI and arms control are antithetical, but the evidence points in the opposite direction.

What Do the Soviets Really Think?

Soviet actions provide ample grounds for believing that Soviet concerns and perceptions are not exactly what they would have us believe. Even though the themes of Soviet public statements are shaped by propagandists this does not, however, explain what the Soviet leadership really thinks about SDI. Moreover, the United States should continue to seek a better understanding of true Soviet perceptions, for these can affect the Soviet willingness to engage in a cooperative approach to greater defense reliance.

The Soviets have superiority in conventional forces and a geographic advantage on the Eurasian land mass. In the nuclear strategic realm they have a significant numerical advantage over the United States in prompt, hard target kill capability from their large ICBMs. Finally, they have a centralized planning apparatus free of democratic constraints which allows them to rapidly rechannel resources in desired directions. They were quite satisfied with the pre-SDI imbalance in strategic defense activities between the United States and USSR. They see little advantage in moving cooperatively to a more defense-reliant regime since their current advantages in both offense and defense would be reduced or balanced. However, Soviet attitudes regarding intermediate range nuclear forces seem to be changing. The Soviets were quite content during the period when they enjoyed a monopoly in LRINF missiles. Now that the US has started to deploy such missiles, the Soviets appear more willing to negotiate limits.

I believe that the Soviets are genuinely nervous about a concerted allied effort to explore applying exotic technologies to strategic defense systems. This concern derives in part from their deep respect for the sophistication of past US space and other technological efforts. The Soviets may fear that the marriage of Western technological genius and American space expertise could lead to US dominance in the military uses of space. Even though the Soviets boast about their ability to overcome any future space-based defenses, they seem to fear Western advances in SDI.

I do not believe that the Soviets see a hidden agenda in SDI such as US acquisition of a space-based ground attack capability. The Soviets know what kind of systems are being researched in the SDI program. They know that those systems effective in an SDI ballistic missile defense would be highly optimized for this purpose, and would be unsuitable for attacks on ground targets. They also realize that the United States is developing new offensive systems in its strategic modernization program which are directed toward ground targets and will be quite suitable for that deterrent mission as long as is necessary. My skepticism about Soviet seriousness on this point has been reinforced by private conversations with those who should know Soviet views.

The Soviet negotiators in the defense and space talks have expressed little interest in the cooperative transition concept. I believe this reluctance reflects less the view that such a transition could not work, and more the view that even to engage in discussions at this point would undermine the Soviet position on "space-strike arms."

The Soviets are skeptical that the United States might deliberately introduce future strategic defenses in such a way that neither side would gain unilateral advantage. To remove Soviet doubts will require consistency and perseverance on the part of US policy-makers and negotiators. We are therefore prepared for serious discussions with the Soviets about the process of introducing strategic defenses which would provide each side increased security against attack.

Conclusion

Our hope is that the US SDI research program will start an historic transition to a world in which the most sophisticated technologies are applied against weapons of mass destruction rather than against people. We are under no illusions that this transition will be either short or easy.

On the Soviet side, there must be a change in both tactics and substance. The easiest step for the Soviets would be to begin serious discussion of defense and space issues, including abandoning the propagandistic expressions about "space-strike arms" and "militarization of space" and starting to discuss these issues with precision. It also means that the Soviets must abandon the pretense that they have no counterpart to the US SDI research effort.

Another step would be for the Soviets to reverse the erosion in the ABM Treaty caused by their non-compliant activities. Such a step could have a very beneficial impact on the US-Soviet relationship and on prospects for the nuclear and space arms talks.

Finally, the Soviets should address the legitimate security concerns of the United States and its allies. Soviet advantages in strategic offensive and defensive systems are a reality today. Soviet complaints about potential future US superiority in strategic defensive systems describe a future which the United States does not seek and which the Soviets say they will not allow to occur. We accept that the Soviets, like ourselves, have concerns about one-sided advances in the strategic forces of the other. We are willing to continue to address the legitimate security concerns of the Soviet Union, but we expect their reciprocity.

Paul H. Nitze was *Special Adviser to the President and Secretary of State on Arms Control Matters. Ambassador Nitze has held numerous positions in government to include head of the US Negotiating Team, Arms Control and Disarmament Agency, Geneva (1981-84); Member of the US Delegation, Strategic Arms Limitation Talks (1969-74); Deputy Secretary of Defense (1967-69); Secretary of the Navy (1963-67); Assistant Secretary of Defense for International*

Security Affairs (1961-63). At the Department of State he also served as Director, Policy Planning Staff (1950-53); Deputy to Assistant Secretary of State for Economic Affairs (1948-49); and Deputy Director of the Office of International Trade Policy (1946). Earlier he was Director, then Vice Chairman, US Strategic Bombing Survey (1944-46).

Ambassador Nitze holds a B.A. degree from Harvard University and LL.D. degrees from the New School of Social Research, Pratt Institute, and John Hopkins. He has contributed articles to Foreign Policy, *the* Reporter, *the* New York Times, *and other publications and is the author of* US Foreign Policy, 1945-1955 *(Foreign Policy Association, 1956) and* Securing the Seas: Soviet Naval Challenge and Western Alliance Options (Boulder, CO: Westview Press, 1979).

PART II

US DOCTRINE AND FORCE STRUCTURE

IS THE AIR DEFENSE PROBLEM BYPASSING THE SDI?

Peter A. Wilson

As the strategic nuclear competition enters an environment of increasingly effective ballistic missile defense, the importance of aerodynamic attack systems will increase. Currently, the Soviets have a very vigorous program to develop and deploy a wide range of manned and unmanned aerodynamic nuclear attack systems, including a new generation of strategic bombers and long-range cruise missiles. Irrespective of any US decision to deploy ballistic missile defense systems, the Soviets have powerful military motives to develop and deploy an increasingly diverse aerodynamic attack capability. This essay will explore briefly the status of current Soviet programs, their possible missions, and suggest future system concepts that may appear by 2000—as well as plausible US air defense options.

The Current Programs

Public literature reveals that Soviet deployment of advanced aerodynamic attack systems is well underway. The major elements of these programs are as follows:[1]

Two new classes of long-range cruise missiles

- A Tomahawk class subsonic missile which includes an air-launched cruise missile (ALCM) variant, the AS-15, a sea-launched cruise missile (SLCM) variant, the SS-NX-21, and a ground-launched cruise missile (GLCM) variant, the SSC-X-4.[2]

- A large supersonic cruise missile which includes a SLCM variant, the SS-NX-24; an ALCM variant, the AS-X- 16, may be deployed.

- A variety of advanced supersonic air-to-surface missiles which appear as follow-ons to the supersonic AS-4/6 ASMs, the AS-X-16.[3]

Two new strategic bombers

- The new production variant of the subsonic *Bear* bomber, the *Bear* H which is the current carrier of the AS-15 ALCM.
- A B-1B class supersonic bomber, the *Blackjack*.

During the next five years, considerable uncertainty exists concerning the precise direction and velocity of these programs. Currently, the most immediate new aerodynamic threat to North America is the *Bear* H armed with the AS-15. Published reports indicate that the Soviets have a vigorous production program with more than 60 currently deployed. Estimates are that the *Bear* H will carry six AS-15s internally with an additional four or six carried under wing pylons. Thus, the Soviets are rapidly deploying a capability that matches the US B-52 force armed with the ALCM-B.[4]

Coupled with the build-up of the *Bear* H fleet, the Soviet air force has introduced a vigorous training program, including flights off the coast of Greenland, Alaska, and the Canadian arctic. These exercises suggest the Soviets are committed to building a large force which may well reach more than 100 aircraft by the early 1990s. Thus North America may soon face an ALCM threat of well over 1,000 weapons. Although the subsonic *Bear* is not a demanding air defense target, the AS-15 will challenge any contemporary air defense system. Its range approximates that of our ALCM-B, approximately 3,000 kilometers; it will fly at low altitudes to avoid ground-based radar detection. Furthermore, the vehicle presents a modest radar cross section which will stress the detection capability of many current early warning and airborne fire control radars.

The second active program is the Soviet testing of the SLCM variant of the AS-15, the SS-NX-21. Similar to the *Tomahawk*, this SLCM can be launched from the torpedo tube of a modern submarine. Strong expectations are that the SS-NX-21 will be deployed on the current generation of modern Soviet SSNs, such as the *Victor* III. Right now the Soviets have 20 of these modern

SSNs. In addition, the lead boats of several new SSN classes are being developed, including the *Akula* and *Sierra* SSNs.[5] If the Soviets chose to deploy the SS-NX-21 on various modern SSNs, the resulting combination of a "stealthy" cruise and quiet submarine will present the United States with a worrisome new threat.

Another possibility is that the Soviets might deploy forward numerous modern SLCM-armed SSNs off the coast of the United States. This tactic would stress the Navy's current ASW surveillance system.[6] Furthermore, it would seriously challenge the air surveillance system since the SLCMs could be launched at the likely gaps in the low-altitude coverage of the current land-based radar system, the Joint Surveillance System (JSS). In theory, such forward-deployed SLCMs could be direct threats to critical command nodes of the National Command Authority (NCA) and the main operating bases for SAC bombers and tankers. Such Soviet theoretical "precursor or leading edge" attack concepts could soon present a serious threat. In fact, the Soviets have suggested that such a forward deployment was to be a "response" to the US deployment of Pershing II and GLCM into Europe. Until last year, various Soviet commentators gave this threat considerable prominence. However, because INF negotiations progressed to a Treaty in 1988, that immediate threat has become moot. Further, there is no public evidence that the Soviets have actually forward deployed SSNs in a steady state mode off the coast of the continental United States (CONUS). In fact, such deployment would contradict the current strategy of smiles which the Gorbachev regime is vigorously pursuing.

Two other Soviet aerodynamic programs continue, but have future operational deployment dates. The first is the *Blackjack* variable geometry supersonic bomber, an oversized version of our B-1. As the Soviet R&D effort continues, we can expect the *Blackjack* will be deployed in limited numbers by the mid-1990s. Soviet public commentary suggests that it will be armed with the AS-15, but it may well be equipped with a wide range of advanced ASMs (some of which are anti-ship) and act as a very long-range variant of the multi-mission *Backfire*. Given its very high production costs, it is unlikely that the Soviets will deploy the *Blackjack* only as an ALCM "truck" for the AS-15, a mission already ably performed by the *Bear* H.

The other active program is the large supersonic cruise missile, the SS-NX-24, which is currently being tested from a modified *Yankee* class SSBN. Possibly, the Soviets will convert a number of the demobilized *Yankees* to carry this long-range weapon, but wide-scale deployment will likely await a new generation of SSBNs which have improved underwater characteristics.[7] From the US planners' perspective, the SS-NX-24 may prove to be a less worrisome problem than the SS-NX-21 since its propulsion system works best at supersonic high-altitude flight, hardly a "stealthy" profile. On the other hand, the SS-NX-24 may be more worrisome if its propulsion system eventually permits both low- and high-altitude flight. Given its larger payload, non-nuclear variants (for anti-ship and land attack) of the 24 could possibly appear by the early 1990s.

Unlike the SS-NX-21, the SS-NX-24 will require a specialized launch tube; thus its deployment is clearly linked to specialized submarines. The SS-NX-21, being compatible with a torpedo tube, could be placed on a wide range of modern nuclear and non-nuclear powered submarines. Further, the Soviets may well disguise their SS-NX-21 submarines; only missile test activity would reveal the threat.

In summary, much uncertainty will remain concerning the scale of the Soviet SLCM and ALCM deployments. The only certain element as of 1988 is the deployment of a large *Bear* H force equipped with the AS-15. However, one should not be surprised if the Soviets continue to significantly expand their commitment to aerodynamic attack systems. In fact, several powerful arguments favor such a substantial program.

Soviet Motivation

Although a Soviet build-up of aerodynamic forces is a likely response to any US unilateral deployment of ballistic missile defenses, they have other equal and more persuasive motives for a substantial program. The first is nuclear force diversification, a broadening of the Soviet nuclear "triad," and the second is an emulation strategy which can act as a bargaining tool during the ongoing arms negotiations. The third is continuing to exploit advanced aerodynamic attack systems, to provide for increasingly ambitious non-nuclear theater and global warfighting missions.

Force Diversification. The most powerful argument favoring the current Soviet aerodynamic attack program is a military decision to exploit new nuclear technologies which will assure Soviet retaliation and warfighting potential. Until the late 1970s, the Soviet military appeared comfortable with a nuclear force dominated by the fixed silo-based ICBMs. Approximately 70 percent of the Soviet nuclear offensive potential resided in these ICBM forces. Most of the remaining nuclear firepower was in the SSBN fleet increasingly equipped with ICBM-range SLBMs. Such an SSBN posture assured a nuclear reserve even if the hardened ICBM force could be threatened by US nuclear forces.

From the Soviet perspective, such diversification now seems insufficient, particularly as US antisubmarine warfare capabilities have evolved. A modernized Soviet strategic bomber force could prove a plausible hedge to Soviet concerns about their fixed-ICBM vulnerability and not-so-hidden SLBM force. Thus, during the late 1970s, Soviet military leaders pressed ahead with a variety of mobile ICBM programs, chiefly the SS-25 and SS-24 ICBMs. As with bombers which can be quickly launched on tactical warning, mobile ICBMs make any US investment in accurate hard-target-kill MIRV and advanced ASW systems less militarily significant. Another factor influencing Soviet aerodynamic upgrade has been the clear evidence of the United States in the last 20 years to disinvest in air defense systems.

Weak US Air Defenses. Once the United States decided not to invest in huge ABM systems, it, unlike the Soviet Union, consciously gave up major efforts to deploy a modern continental air defense. US decision-makers viewed this situation as quite "rational" since the build-up of Soviet nuclear offensive power was concentrated in an expanding force of ICBMs. All advanced aerodynamic defense systems were cancelled or reoriented toward a theater warfighting mission. For example, the Mach 3 F-12 interceptor was not deployed—only its reconnaissance variant, the SR-71. All strategic surface-to-air missile systems, such as the *Nike-Hercules*, were phased out. Its follow-on, the much-delayed *Patriot* has been deployed only as a theater defense system. In a similar fashion, the main rationale for the E-3 *Sentry*, Airborne Warning and Control System (AWACS) was primarily as an offensive system for directing theater warfighting. Thus, a continental air defense evolved into a thin area "coast guard" of the air.

Soviet military planners noticed this potential opportunity to place the United States at risk. Having mastered the long-range subsonic missile technology analogous to the *Tomahawk*, the Soviets embarked upon a build-up of an ALCM carrier fleet. Some observers were surprised when the Soviets resumed production of a variant of the TU-95 *Bear* intercontinental bomber. However, the Soviets had the clear precedent of the United States revitalizing its B-52 fleet in a similar conversion to ALCM carriers. Furthermore, the outcome of the SALT-II negotiations may have played an important role in stimulating a revival of the Soviet bomber force.

The United States was quite successful in protecting its ALCM program by negotiating modest constraints on their deployment, using the "averaging" rule. At the time, only the United States could exploit this weak constraint on deploying ALCMs on strategic bombers.

The Soviets knew that the United States would gain a powerful unilateral advantage by deploying very large numbers of ALCMs, based upon the *Tomahawk* class technology of the USAF's ACLM-B missile. Thus, the *Bear* H and AS-15 combination likely resulted from a Soviet need to find a quick bargaining counter to the US program which would be fully mature during the early 1980s phase of the arms control negotiations. As suggested, the weak US air defense system influenced a Soviet decision to rapidly expand its nuclear aerodynamic strike potential, especially if they could not easily constrain US aerodynamic programs during the START era of the arms negotiations. In addition, the Soviet General Staff may have considered the need to upgrade the Soviet Union's deep non-nuclear strike potential.

The Non-Nuclear Shift in Strategy. Although this essay does not address conventional systems, considerable evidence shows a profound Soviet political/military shift away from a world war scenario dominated by early and massive use of nuclear weapons. Since the late 1970s, the Soviet High Command has continually emphasized the development and deployment of substantial non-nuclear warfighting capabilities.[8] A strong case has been made that the Soviet military now plans to fight a prolonged non-nuclear war against the Atlantic Alliance—the objective being to defeat the European allies and expel the United States from Eurasia. During this conflict, the Soviets would rely on their diverse and survivable nuclear forces to paralyze NATO's attempt to begin nuclear combat operations in the critical Central Front of Europe.[9]

Consistent with this strategy is a Soviet need to deploy increasingly effective long-range, non-nuclear strike systems. We should not be surprised that we now see a major Soviet investment in long-range aviation, designed to support both combined arms operations in Eurasia as well as deep naval operations. Of note is the Soviet deployment of supersonic *Backfire* bombers with both land attack and anti-ship missions. Currently, the Soviets are deploying the *Bear* bomber fleet with both missions in mind. The *Bear* H is armed with the nuclear variant of the AS-15 ALCM. Another variant is the *Bear* G which carries the AS-4, a high-performance, anti-ship missile. Quite likely, the longer-range *Blackjack* will have similar multi-mission requirements and capabilities. In addition, the Soviets may deploy non-nuclear variants of the AS-15, as well as other advanced land-attack, precision-guided missiles.

Long-range aircraft could attack a variety of critical land targets important to NATO's Atlantic reinforcement potential, including critical facilities in the United Kingdom and Iceland. In the future, key targets could be located in North America. The Soviets would wish to disrupt the US capacity to reinforce Europe as well as support the forward elements of the *Maritime Strategy*. The latter operational concept posits a vigorous US naval campaign against Soviet naval bastions in the Barents Sea and the North Pacific. This operational concept includes possible non-nuclear missile and air attacks on key Soviet naval facilities. In response to such attacks, the Soviets could choose to escalate "horizontally" with long-range air attacks on key NATO targets in Alaska, Canada, and possibly CONUS. The latter possibility could become a reality if the Soviets were able to counter air surveillance facilities in the Arctic region. Many ground-based radar sites, such as elements of Space Command's Northern Warning System, are vulnerable to non-nuclear attack with precision-guided, stand-off missiles.

From the Soviet perspective, long-range aviation could counter some of the more ambitious elements of the *Maritime Strategy*. Unlike long-range ballistic missile systems, the Soviets could employ their bomber force on repeated sorties to attack a variety of NATO targets at great "operational" depth. Armed with the appropriate long-range stand-off weapons, even the subsonic *Bear* might prove a formidable strike platform. Furthermore, public evidence suggests that the Soviets will use their advanced SU-27 as a long-range fighter escort for deep bomber missions. Such fighter escorts would make sense during a non-nuclear campaign which called for multiple bomber sorties.[10]

The foregoing analysis suggests that Soviet interest in expanding and modernizing its "strategic" bomber fleet is substantial irrespective of what happens regarding early deployment of SDI.

In response to this modernized aerodynamic threat, the United States has begun to upgrade its own air defense capability.

United States Near-Term Air Defense Response

The United States has chiefly attempted to upgrade its air defenses by improving its capacity to detect low cross-section cruise missile systems. Experts agree that the current system of ground-based micro-wave class surveillance radars can be bypassed by low-flying small radar cross-section aircraft and missiles. The current program consists of the following elements:

The Joint Surveillance System (JSS). The United States has upgraded its CONUS ground-based radar and control system. The system uses both military and FAA-controlled radars to provide improved medium- and high-altitude radar coverage over the United States. As with all ground-based radars, such coverage deteriorates line-of-sight limitations against low-flying targets (e.g., below 100 meters above ground level (AGL)).

The Northern Warning System (NWS) represents an upgrade of the Distant Early Warning (DEW line) ground-based radar systems. This system includes the recently deployed minimally manned high performance radars in Alaska (Igloo Program) and 15 other sites as part of the NWS. The larger GE radars, AN/FPS-117, will be supplemented by 39 unmanned "gapfillers" built by

Sperry. The latter will see full deployment by the early 1990s. When completed, the NWS will provide a state-of-the-art arctic radar barrier, extending from Alaska to the Canadian northeast coast and across Greenland.

Over-the-Horizon Backscatter (OTH-B) Radar. The most significant new aerodynamic sensor is the over-the-horizon radar, with the first site becoming fully operational in early 1990. These radar operate in the HF frequency band and use the ionosphere as a refractive medium to provide very long-range coverage against large aircraft. The OTH-B has a maximum range of approximately 3,000 kilometers and a minimum range of 900 kilometers. The latter constraint because of the minimum range imposed by the height of the ionosphere and the refractive angle possible with an HF signal. Hopefully, the low frequency of the HF radar will improve the capacity to detect a low radar cross section (e.g., "stealthy" targets). The United States Air Force plans a series of tests to confirm the experimental and theoretical potential of the OTH-B to detect small cruise missiles with the first radar sector during the winter of 1988.[11]

The ultimate plan is to deploy a west coast three-radar system, followed by a two-radar system for Alaska and four-radar system for interior CONUS. The latter will provide a southward facing coverage, plus coverage inside the minimum range of the east and west coast sites. If budgets permit, the total system will be operational by the mid-1990s.[12]

The OTH-B is attractive because it provides very wide area coverage from a relatively small number of sites. On the other hand, the system has some important operational limitations. The effectiveness of the HF radar is critically dependent upon the ionosphere's status which changes radically from night to day. Further, it is profoundly affected by solar activity or the lack thereof. Thus, the wide area radar coverage will have some of the drawbacks of wide area ASW surveillance systems which are critically dependent upon changes in the oceanic environment. Hence, some sort of airborne radar must provide dynamic coverage especially when the OTH-B is "down" for adverse environmental reasons. Given the geometry and character of the ionosphere, this situation will more likely occur during nighttime operations.

Improved Airborne Early Warning (AEW) Aircraft. During the early 1980s, the United States Air Force had hoped to acquire an additional eight E-3 Airborne Warning and Control Systems to supplement the current fleet of 34 aircraft. These aircraft would be dedicated to the CONUS air defense mission. However, budgetary constraints and doubts about the E-3A's operational limitations led to a program cancellation. Currently, the air defense community is looking at AWACS follow-ons, such as long-endurance and high-flying (20,000 meter-plus altitude) manned and unmanned platforms, as well as large airships. The United States Navy had considered releasing monies to develop a large AEW airship, equipped with a large low-frequency radar. Unfortunately that program was cancelled during the winter of 1988 because of budgetary constraints.[13]

Related to the airship is the aerostat concept of "flying" a radar in a tethered large streamlined balloon. Currently, three are operational, two in Florida and one in the Bahamas. As part of an anti-drug smuggling initiative, plans call for deploying five similar systems along the Mexican and US border over the next two years.[14] The aerostat is attractive since it provides an airborne radar platform at a fraction of the cost of maintaining AEW aircraft in orbit. Unfortunately, the aerostat is vulnerable to severe weather, especially lightning; therefore, it is no panacea for providing absolutely reliable low-altitude coverage against small aircraft and/or missiles.

Aside from improvements in radar coverage, the United States is investing modestly to upgrade its active air defense forces. Originally, the USAF wanted to replace its active and National Guard squadrons, currently equipped with obsolescent F-106 and F-4 interceptors, with the F-15. Budgets have not permitted this upgrade, and the current plan calls for replacing them with a modified variant of 270 early model F-16s. This program should be complete by the early 1990s.

Aside from the F-16 upgrade program, no near-term plans are underway to improve the active air defense forces although various tactical fighter units might provide enhanced air defense coverage during a crisis. Deployments could include additional F-16s, more capable USAF F-15s, and USN/USMC F-14s and F-18s. Of note, Canada's contribution to active air defense has improved considerably since its air force now has the F-18, an aircraft with a very respectable look down/shoot down capability.

Beyond these initiatives, future US upgrades remain quite uncertain. The most important future focus is the Air Defense Initiative (ADI), the aerodynamic complement to SDI. ADI is a relatively modestly funded program for exploring future air defense technology and options which would complement a deployed ballistic missile defense system of the late 1990s. Many unknowns must be resolved before the ADI leads to concrete programs with plausible procurement schedules. These unknowns include forecasts of the Soviet aerodynamic threat, SDI, technology breakthroughs, and, above all, future funding. Any new substantial ADI programs will likely face severe budgetary pressure for the next decade.[15] Without a powerful internal stimulus, the national debate over defense spending will likely see protracted slow growth and federal budget deficits well into the 1990s. As for the evolving Soviet threat, some interesting possibilities exist.

Possible Soviet Options

Before discussing possible Soviet "strategic" developments in aerodynamic weapons, we should note that the Gorbachev regime faces many daunting economic and national security choices. That regime has indicated a strong desire to slow down the current military-technological competition with the industrial democracies. For the next five to ten years, the Gorbachev regime will probably constrain the rate of increase in military investment.[16] To modernize the Soviet economy is an enormous task and will require massive and sustained capital investment. Without squeezing consumption, which would further hamper an increase in labor productivity, the Soviet leadership will likely cut back on military expenditures.

True, the Soviets will continue to devote very large resources to the military, especially in high technology sectors. Insofar as new aerodynamic systems are concerned, some programs may suffer for both technical and budgetary reasons. On the other hand, the Soviets will likely be able to deploy a new generation of aerodynamic attack systems by the mid- to late-1990s as my essay has earlier pointed out. More specifically, the size and mix of the *Bear* H and *Blackjack* programs are noteworthy. Current public evidence suggests that the *Bear* H program is very vigorous and will lead to a 100 aircraft deployment by 1990. By the early 1990s, the US will face a "minimum" threat of 1,000 AS-15s from a fully generated *Bear* H force.

The *Blackjack* program remains uncertain as to actual deployment and ultimate fleet size. By the mid-1990s, a fleet of some 100 aircraft is plausible; these aircraft may well have multiple missions similar to the shorter range *Backfire*, currently deployed in almost equal numbers between the Soviet air force and naval aviation units. Because the *Blackjack* has a supersonic dash capability, we should expect to see it armed with a wide variety of air-launched stand-off weapons, including the AS-15. These new stand-off weapons may well be non-nuclear variants of the AS-15, AS-4, and a Soviet version of the GBU-15 electro-optically guided bomb.

Another interesting question is whether the Soviets will deploy a large tanker fleet during the 1990s.

Currently, the Soviets are developing a tanker version of the IL-76 transport. Given the age of the current tanker fleet (converted *Mya*-4 bombers), the Soviets may well undertake a substantial modernization. Similar to the United States, the Soviets could deploy a large tanker fleet for both their bomber and long-range interceptor force. On the other hand, the Soviets traditionally do not give high priority to an aerial tanker fleet. Again, resource constraints and competing modernization priorities may slow Soviet tanker deployment.

Other mid-1990s' options are worth watching, particularly the possible widespread deployment of the naval variant of the AS-15, the SS-N-21. Looking at possible future arms control agreements, the Soviets might find the argument for a large SS-N-21 force compelling. Because of their modest size, arms control constraints on the *Tomahawk* class cruise missile may be limited. If future arms control constraints reduce larger ballistic missile inventories, then the relative worth of varied cruise missile systems will increase accordingly. Furthermore, the Soviet Navy has a powerful operational argument for deploying SS-N-21s on its new generation of quiet SSNs, namely to diversify the "strategic" nuclear threat to the United States. More specifically, the deep-ocean deployment of modern SSNs, equipped with long-range cruise missiles, will strain the US Navy's ASW assets and dilute the operational effectiveness of an anti-SSBN strategy, now central to the *Maritime Strategy*.

Later in the 1990s, the Soviets may deploy non-nuclear variants of the SS-N-21 or the large SS-NX-24. These weapons could be used in distant power-projection missions or play a role in an "all azimuth" air operation against Eurasian targets.

All the potential missions for the sea-launched cruise missile suggest the United States may well face a substantial SLCM threat to CONUS, irrespective of any Soviet interest in the US C³I system with a "leading edge" type attack. In theory, quiet SSNs, armed with a stealthy cruise missile and deployed off the coasts of

CONUS, could stress the US warning system. However, current evidence indicates the Soviets lack strong interest in this option because of the politically provocative message that a steady-state, close-in deployment would send. Still, the Soviets might consider such a deployment during a high-crisis maneuver, which could place the US NCA under stress.

Aside from SLCM deployments, the other interesting possibility is a *Backfire/Fencer* follow-on which has "stealth" characteristics. Certainly, the Soviets have a long-standing requirement to replace one or both aircraft with a Red version of the A-12, the Advanced Tactical Aircraft (ATA) (which the Navy sees as the A-6 replacement). Although this aircraft may lack sufficient range to be a direct CONUS threat, a stealth threat is certainly plausible by 2000.

Early 21st-Century Threats

Given the history of technological innovation, the secrets of stealth will not remain the unique province of the United States. Over time the Soviets could develop varied low-observable missile systems. The first might well be the follow-on to the AS-15, a Red Advanced Cruise Missile (ACM), designed to upgrade the *Bear* H and *Blackjack* fleet. Another possibility is an intercontinental cruise missile (ICCM) based on a ground-mobile transporter erector launcher (TEL). In fact, one can conceptualize a multi-stage ICCM having intercontinental range. The first "stage" could be a long-endurance vehicle,[17] designed to defeat airborne and space-based wide-area surveillance systems. The second "stage" could be a small "micro" missile, deployable to defeat terminal surveillance and defense fire-control systems. Depending on how the arms control process and the status of SDI evolve, the Soviets might deploy numerous ICCMs in dispersed and hidden sites. This tactic would assure a large retaliation force, even if the missiles took many hours to reach their target.

To provide a very high-quality defense against this type of threat, the ADI would have to possess some sophisticated surveillance and kill mechanisms.

Possible ADI Systems

Current publicity suggests that "stealth" does not make objects invisible; instead, it radically degrades the performance of microwave radar systems. Further evidence suggests that small radar-cross-section targets can be detected, using very large-aperture, low-frequency radars—especially those operating in the UHF band.[18] For this reason, the US Navy has shown renewed interest in the airship. By the fall of 1987, the Navy had contracted with Airship International and Westinghouse to build a prototype AEW airship. A prototype was to fly by the early 1990s. The airship concept is attractive because airships have very long endurance and low operating costs, compared to a conventional fixed-wing AEW aircraft. From operational experience, both the US Air Force and US Navy have discovered the very high costs of maintaining AEW aircraft in sustained airborne orbits. The USAF experience with its Saudi Arabian-based E-3s is a useful case in point.

In fact, if no plausible competitor is forthcoming by the early 1990s, the United States Air Force might get over the so-called "giggle factor" and actually buy variants of the airship. A fleet of them would nicely complement the OTH-B system which, as we have seen, faces transient but steady operational degradation. Furthermore, the air force could deploy several airships off the CONUS coasts to operate near Soviet cruise missile armed SSNs once they are detected by the Navy's wide area ASW surveillance system. This combination of US sensors would likely hinder Soviet interest in deploying cruise missiles as part of a "leading edge" attack option. Unfortunately this concept has died once again as the Navy has cancelled the R&D effort. In theory, the Defense Advanced Research Projects Agency (DARPA) will develop the concept, but there is little funding for a credible R&D program.

For a variety of reasons, the United States Air Force could invest in other long-endurance sensor platform concepts, including very-high-flying TR-1 class aircraft (manned or unmanned) equipped with a confirmal UHF radar. This latter technology is likely to mature by the early 1990s. The aircraft would operate at six times the altitude of an airship and provide substantially greater low-altitude coverage of small radar targets. Although more expensive to operate than an airship, these aircraft might well be worthwhile since a smaller fleet size would give equivalent sensor coverage.

Before developing a "high flyer," the USAF might consider an intermediate solution, such as the Lockheed proposal to fly a very large-aperture side-looking radar on a C-130.[19] Even though the C-130 will lack the endurance advantages of the airship, the air force might well have the C-130 supplement the E-3 in a joint sur-veillance role. Both aircraft can be deployed forward to Eurasian theaters of operation. If the non-nuclear cruise missile threat to NATO targets becomes severe by the mid-1990s, deploying airborne platforms (capable of detecting such small targets) may be a very reasonable solution.

Looking beyond the next generation of airborne AEW platforms, space-based sensors may offer a distinct possibility. Options include space-based radar and infrared concepts. The space-based radar (SBR) concept was seen as a panacea to the air surveillance problem during the late 1970s and early 1980s. However, tech-nological, operational, and cost problems have pre-vented any near-term deployment. The basic problem with the space-based radar is the inverse square law which requires geometrically greater power and aper-ture to detect targets at ever greater orbital altitudes. Current technology suggests that space-based radar can detect large aircraft at altitudes of several thousand kilo-meters. However, the detection of small radar targets require developing a second generation of space radar technology which will not be available until 2000.

In addition, the SBR satellite presents a large and lucrative target to a variety of ASAT threats. Thus, SBR will need a heavy defense and will be vulnerable during a major war. The USAF's Project Forecast II suggests more exotic concepts, such as distributed arrays in orbit which would be more damage resistant. Clearly, possibilities exist for the next century, but they bring with them substantial technological and cost challenges.

Passive detection systems are also possible, such as the much-delayed *Teal Ruby* program—an airborne sensor program for detecting aircraft flying at medium and high altitudes. However, another generation of "starring" intermediate range (IR) sensors is necessary for detecting very small IR targets (e.g., cruise missiles operating at low altitude and subsonic velocities). Considerable technological uncertainty remains about whether such sensors can be deployed to provide long-range detection. On the other hand, long-range cruise missiles will require many hours to reach their target and could be detected, especially when operating outside cloud cover.

As in the case of the SBR, a space-based IR air defense sensor will be vulnerable to ASAT attack. In theory, the space-based elements of an early SDI could defend these sensors. In any event, wide deployment of space-based sensors for offensive and defensive missions will profoundly affect the nature of any hypothetical global war fought at the turn of the century. By 2000, a clear need will exist to acquire a "space combat" capability to destroy an opponent's sensors before launching long-range ballistic and aerodynamic attack weapons. In essence, a space combat phase could well precede the launching of any offensive nuclear weapons from mobile and hidden platforms waiting for an "all clear."

Besides detecting and tracking aerodynamic targets, there will be the problem of killing such targets. One clear consequence of stealth technology will be the increased difficulty for air defense to kill targets with non-nuclear warheads. Stealth will be most effective against manned and unmanned interceptors which employ radar-guided weapons to attack the intruder. Wide area surveillance is feasible, using high power and low frequency radars, but these radars lack the high frequency and smaller aperture sensors adequate to guide weapons to targets.[20]

One possibility is employing "high brightness" directed-energy weapons which should be available by 2000. In this sense, investing in second-generation SDI systems may provide a very potent air defense weapon. Initially, high altitude aircraft will be vulnerable to space-based energy weapons. Further in the future, it may be possible to attack targets operating near the earth's surface. However, right now, such prediction is highly speculative. Exotic energy weapon technologies will evolve but they will be dominated by political and economic factors during the late 1980s and early 1990s. An arms control agreement which severely limits the deployment of space combat systems is certainly possible, especially if both superpowers conclude that the speed of high technology arms competition must be slowed during the early 1990s. Also, as we have noted, both the United States and the Soviet Union will experience severe economic constraints well into the 1990s— constraints which will limit the scale of R&D in advanced energy weapons. On the other hand, the recent breakthroughs in superconductivity may profoundly alter the "economics" of directed energy weapons.

Overall considerable uncertainty remains as to whether air defense options will mature very rapidly during the next 10 to 15 years.

Conclusion

If the United States presses ahead with a major ballistic missile defense program intended to limit damage during a large nuclear attack, an air defense complement will be absolutely necessary. The nuclear aerodynamic threat will likely require an investment that matches defeating the ballistic missile threat. In a purely competitive environment (e.g., no Nitze type deal on joint superpower aerospace defense deployments), the air defense task may well prove more formidable than the daunting objectives articulated by the SDI advocates.

Irrespective of what happens with SDI, the Soviets are likely to invest heavily in aerodynamic attack systems—systems which will present extraordinarily difficult problems for the designer and budgeter of future air defenses. Without a substantial SDI deployment, it is unlikely the United States will invest significantly in ADI type air defense systems. As in the last 20 years, air defense technologies must correspond to tactical and operational requirements. Certainly, the non-nuclear armed cruise missile threat may become a major worry for NATO and other US Eurasian allies by the mid-1990s.

Peter A. Wilson *is a consultant with the RAND Corporation and Los Alamos National Laboratories dealing with national security issues. He has served as a member of the Department of State Policy Planning Staff (1978-81), and as an analyst in the Central Intelligence Agency's Office of Strategic Research (1975-1978). He has written numerous articles on national security matters, including "The Marine Corps in 1985" and "The Marine Corps in 1995" in* US Naval Proceedings. *Other articles include "A Follow-On US Echelon for US NATO Defense" and "The Geo-Strategic Risk of SDI." Mr. Wilson holds a B.A. from Princeton University and an M.A. from the University of Chicago.*

NOTES

1. See pp. 50-53 for details of Soviet aerodynamic programs in: *Soviet Military Power* (Washington, DC: U.S. Government Printing Office, 1988); hereafter *SMP*.

2. GLCM variants were terminated with the INF Treaty going into force during the summer of 1988.

3. More than 45 older *Bear* variants have been converted to carry the AS-4 and possibly the more capable AS-X-16. This variant is known as the *Bear* G.

4. *SMP*, pp. 50-53.

5. Currently both SSNs, in particular the *Akula*, are judged to have dramatically improved acoustic characteristics. Production tempo for both remains slow, one/two boats per annum.

6. *SMP*, pp. 50-53 and pp. 78-79.

7. Recently, a *Yankee* has been converted to carry the SS-N-21. The status of the SS-NX-24 remains murky.

8. See Peter A. Wilson, *A Review of General Purpose Force Issues for the 1990s*, WDRE R-1032/14, The Washington Defense Group, December 1987 for discussion of the Soviet military's shift to a non-nuclear orientation.

9. For an excellent discussion of the Soviet political military evolution away from the nuclear war scenario, see Michael McGuire, *Military Objectives in Soviet Foreign Policy* (Washington, DC: The Brookings Institution, 1987). Also see, Marshal M. A. Gareyev, M. V. Frunze, *Military Theoretician* (Moscow: Voyenizdat, 1985). Mary G. FitzGerald, *Marshal Ogarkov on Modern War: 1977-1985* (Washington, DC: Center for Naval Analyses, March 1986).

10. Derek Wood, "SU-27 Flanker in Service: First Picture," *Janes' Defense Weekly*, 2 May 1987, pp. 808-809. Comments on possible escort role of the SU-27.

11. James W. Canan, "Steady Steps in Strategic C³I," *Air Force* (June 1987), pp. 44-50.

12. This is increasingly unlikely with current budget cuts. Only the west coast site is certain to survive the new period of budgetary austerity. See Ramon Lopez, "The USA Builds Its OTH-B Radar Barrier," *Interavia* (April 1987), pp. 334-335.

13. For a discussion on the Naval Airship Program (NASP), see Floyd D. Kennedy, Jr., "U.S. Naval Aircraft & Missile Developments in 1986," *US Naval Proceedings* (May 1987), pp. 84 and 263.

14. Aerostat barriers may well be extended from Texas to Florida. Thus, low altitude radar coverage will be greatly enhanced in the southern part of the US.

15. For all practical purposes the ADI had been reduced to a series of modest conceptual and technical studies.

16. Recent evidence suggests that the Gorbachev regime faces a near-term crisis of confidence with continued poor economic performance. For a discussion of the relationship between economic performance and national security, see Richard Cohen and Peter A. Wilson, "Superpowers in Decline?" *Comparative Strategy*, Vol. 7, No. 2 (1988).

17. The unducted fan (UDF) appears very attractive as a long endurance and efficient propulsion system for long-range cruise missiles.

18. For a wide-ranging discussion of "stealth" technology, see Bill Sweetman, "Stealth Aircraft," *Motorbooks International, 1986*, especially Chapter 3, pp. 31-58. For discussions about utility of low frequency radars as "anti-stealth" measures, see Bill Sweetman, "And Now the Stealth-Defeating Radar!" *Interavia* (April 1987), pp. 331-333.

19. Edward H. Kolcum, "Lockheed-Georgia Seeking Major Role in ADI Development," *Aviation Week and Space Technology* (May 18, 1987), pp. 126-127.

20. Sweetman, op. cit., "Stealth Aircraft," Chapter 3.

SUPPORTING THE TRANSITION TO A STRATEGIC DEFENSE

Jack H. Nunn

In discussing the support necessary to change to a strategic defense, we must first note that the Strategic Defense Initiative (SDI) is not a weapons development program, but a research program designed to determine the feasibility of using new technologies for developing a defense against ballistic missiles. However, if the research is successful and a ballistic missile defense is ultimately deployed, such a system will fundamentally change strategic concepts and doctrine. SDI will certainly affect arms control, force posture (both strategic and conventional), and military operational concepts. Those changes, and their effects on the security of the United States and its allies, are the focus of this book.

Previous essays have addressed both the current SDI program and possible Soviet responses. Our assessment of possible Soviet actions, as well as how we evaluate the ultimate feasibility of the technologies, will certainly influence what the United States finally decides about a strategic defense. However, the arguments over the Strategic Defense Initiative, and the nature of any deployed strategic defense, now need to be looked at. Arguments abound but can be grouped in four principal areas:

- The structure of future US forces.
- The nature of US doctrine essential to maintaining our national security while facing both technological developments and actions by our opponents.
- The arms control agreements that might enhance security in these new conditions.
- The actual resources that should be devoted to strategic defense.

In fact, these arguments are already underway. In the research and development field questions have arisen about the amount of funding devoted to SDI and the effects of such funding on other R&D efforts. If we fund a new SDI project, what other R&D projects must the US not fund? Answers to this question ultimately influence force structure and doctrine because R&D decisions close off some long-term options and open others.

In the arms control area questions occur about what tests to conduct and when. What are the pros and cons of early testing? The nature of any deployed system depends, in a key way, on these testing decisions. We certainly will want to test before we "fly" our systems. If so, do we need to make treaty adjustments and if so, how soon? As we move past the R&D phase and toward deployment of a strategic defense, what trade-offs must we consider, based on the arms control process as we have known it to date?

Transition into a deployed defense raises a host of force structure questions. Foremost among these is what are the trade-offs we must make with other strategic programs? For example, given that reduced force vulnerability can come through a number of steps (for example, strategic defense, force dispersal, hardening, and others), should the United States build the small ICBM, or a strategic defense, or both? And what are the trade-offs with conventional forces? Will SDI require, as Dr.Lawrence Korb has indicated,* more conventional forces? Or, will it ultimately require fewer forces? Will a global strategic defense ultimately replace some of these conventional forces? The whole question of how SDI will contribute to our theater capabilities will be a key political issue with our allies as well as a crucial military issue within the Department of Defense.

These critical trade-offs that will occupy our thoughts during any transition period involve tough "resource allocation" problems made tougher by the uncertainties surrounding the technologies and the long

---

*Comments made at American Enterprise Institute, 29 April 1986.

time-line associated with SDI. We are arguing about the effects of a system, the physical nature of which is as yet undefined. However, whatever its final nature, the program, as noted earlier, will draw on significant national resources during both its initial R&D phase and during any future deployment phase. Indeed, a key factor in deploying a strategic defense is developing an *affordable defense*—one that efficiently uses US resources. I want to briefly outline some considerations critical to better understanding the resource issues during a transition to strategic defense.

Structural Impediments to Any Change

Clear impediments stand in the way of *any* change. A change as profound as we are discussing presents great impediments. SDI, as a major new initiative, competes with all other national security programs for scarce defense resources. To compete successfully SDI must: (1) demonstrate how it will operationally replace current national security concepts and doctrines (and improve current security levels); and (2) show how and why its associated hardware (at present largely undefined) will replace over time, some $460 billion worth of hardware either currently planned for, or envisioned, and the expensive hardware currently deployed. Although some of these planned hardware programs are SDI-related (tactical warning and attack assessment upgrades, space defense and operation, etc.), most are oriented toward other missions, some of which may well become obsolete with a deployed strategic defense. There are no clear consensus candidates for elimination. Offensive forces must modernize; so, too, must theater forces. The trade-off between these forces and SDI are complex. How much modernization of offensive forces is necessary? What size will the forces be in a period of offensive/defense mix? What tactical force missions might SDI hardware replace and, therefore, what tactical hardware need not be purchased?

Demonstrating how strategic defense will replace current national security concepts and doctrines will be difficult. All changes in doctrine and force structure involve resource reallocation, but what will be the size and speed of these changes? The natural constituency favoring strategic defense in the United States has always been relatively small. Strategic defense, for example, competes with the Army's principal mission of closing with and defeating the enemy's ground forces, it competes with the Air Force's strategic offensive and theater support missions and forces, and it competes with the Navy's current means of controlling the sea. When it comes to reallocating resources to support this new concept the services will need convincing.

A second major impediment to change is that we are starting with current forces. Any deployment of a strategic defense, any new mix of forces, will be constrained by what we have in place right now. The year 2010, the one targeted in this book, is only some 20 years away. Despite the rapid developments in technology, two decades is not a long time in a military deployment cycle. In 1962, the United States was beginning to deploy our current Minuteman ICBM missile forces; it had B-52s (an older version) and missile submarines. A very large strategic force budget supported this strategic triad. The United States had a major continental air defense force, but it was beginning to reduce that effort. Today, the air defense has all but disappeared, and the other forces have all evolved over time. However, the strategic offensives still play an important military role, and the United States will not get rid of these immediately. This country cannot afford to do so either fiscally or psychologically. As I noted before, those arguing for a strategic defense must show how their proposed operational concepts will improve our national security before we reallocate significant resources to this effort.

Some Key Resource Issues for Consideration

Arguments always can be made against change. My purpose here is not to support such arguments, but to shed light on some of the factors—notably the costs and the validity of the US scientific and industrial base—that will affect that change and shape our world in the 21st century. What must occur in this transition period?

Costs. Resource costs are usually measured in dollars, and it is fashionable to make dollar cost estimates for developing and deploying a strategic defense. However, given the current uncertainty surrounding the physical characteristics of any deployed strategic defense, I will not attempt to make hard dollar estimates because I think they would be premature. Instead, I will focus my remarks on elements of the scientific and industrial base that will be critical to SDI deployment. Whether a deployed system costs $100 billion, $500 billion, or $1 trillion depends not only on what the system looks like, but also on what is done about elements in the US scientific and industrial base. What we need to consider then is the current nature of that base and its potential use.

Scientific and Industrial Base. A fundamental requirement to support any evolution in doctrine and modification of forces from offensive-dominant to some new offensive/defensive mix, is developing a scientific and industrial base (personnel, material, and facilities) which can support the proposed changes. Developing this scientific and industrial base will affect both when a system can be deployed, and how much the system will subsequently cost. The SDIO is aware of the need to establish this baseline (see Lt. Col. Simon P. Worden's opening chapter in Part I, "US Strategic Defense in 2010: A Conjecture" for discussion of costs). General James Abrahamson also has recently addressed the need to develop cost goals for Congress. However, more people need to recognize the critical role of this scientific and industrial base. I would argue that a strategic defense has no chance of deployment unless the current base is developed. For example, deployment of ground-launched interceptors will require expanding propellant production capacity. In addition, the US optics industry is acknowledged to be inadequate for any proposed strategic defense system. Such shortcomings will have to be eliminated if a defense is to be deployed.

A strategic defense deployment will require mobilizing our science and industry, not necessarily in the sense of a World War II mobilization (although such an effort might be necessary if we have a competitive deployment), but we do need a carefully planned and managed approach to develop and produce a significant number of new forces. The mobilization of the scientific base is on-going with new personnel and facilities being assigned research tasks related to strategic defense. Planning for a mobilized industrial base must also begin now if we indeed wish to deploy this strategic defense in the early 21st century. The time requirements associated with the development and deployment of many of the high-technology systems that constitute it are lengthy. For example, we know we will need a robust launch capability (both launcher and launch facilities) for satellites associated with almost all proposed strategic defense architectures. Development of such a capability could take up to a decade. In the wake of the recent launch disasters, we are now only too aware of this need and the problems it entails. In sum, a robust US launch capability and the propellants and optics mentioned earlier are only a few of the areas of US industrial concern; many other areas require study and an organized approach.

Scientific And Industrial Transition. The scientific and industrial transition will be as important and as difficult as the doctrine and force structure transition. The length and nature of a strategic defense development and deployment path are crucial to our assessing actual resource requirements and for developing plans for their efficient use. Obviously numerous development and deployment paths exist. However, in broad terms one can envision an orderly or disorderly transition, a negotiated or competitive deployment, which critics and supporters of SDI have frequently discussed. The speed of any deployment involves a number of trade-offs, even if the deployment is orderly and involves no competition.

The figure below shows two notional research, development, and deployment alternatives for a strategic defense that illustrate some of the resource issues related to our transition to strategic defense. Both alternatives eventually lead to a similarly deployed defensive system. Still, the differing paths probably dictate differing deployment results, and the "full defense" that is finally deployed could have very different capabilities.

Alternative "A" is a research, development, and deployment path with a relatively extended R&D phase. In alternative "A" there would be little actual system deployment during the R&D phase, other than upgrading associated surveillance systems used in offensive tactical warning and attack assessment (TW/AA) missions as technologies mature. Instead, full technologies (mature as well as new) are withheld (and potentially upgraded) until all technical feasibility studies are complete and the feasibility of a total defense system is proven. At that point, a deployment decision is made and the systems rapidly developed.

Alternative "B," on the other hand, represents early deployment of more mature technologies (ground-based terminal defenses, etc.), followed by the deployment of the less mature technologies (space-based directed energy weapons, etc.) as their technical

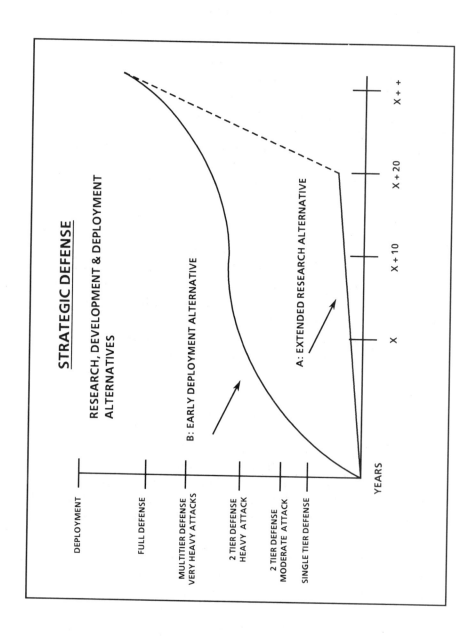

feasibility is proven. Obvious resource trade-offs exist between the two paths. Assuming a constant level of enemy threat (and thus relative constant spending to meet that threat), early deployment will probably reduce the funds available for R&D on the less mature technologies, thus lengthening overall deployment time and potentially leading to a less capable system (or requiring system upgrades of early deployed components to obtain an equivalent system). On the other hand, earlier deployment of mature technologies can reduce the resources required to deploy in any given year (since the deployment is phased over many years), and will provide "hands-on" opportunities to "learn about" a strategic defense system, thus potentially reducing costly mistakes as we deploy it. Further, alternative "B" provides some level of defense capability years before alternative "A." An attempt at too rapid deployment (alternative "A") might overload production facilities. On the other hand, a very slow deployment may increase unit costs. Advantages and disadvantages accompany both alternatives. Accurate planning of resources needed for deployment, and developing the industrial infrastructure to support a deployment, are critical.

The scientific resource problems for either transition path principally involve manpower and some facilities—particularly testing facilities. These will differ, as noted, by the amount of resources being directed at production and deployment. However, in the main, the scientific community must pursue tasks that push at the frontier of knowledge and begin to yield answers to the technical feasibility questions.

The range of problems involving the industrial base is somewhat more complex. Three cases exist. In some cases, an industrial production base will have to be invented—no one, for example, is currently producing particle-beam weapons. If that technology proves to be one chosen for deployment, an industry will have to be constructed from scratch. In other cases, industry will move from a cottage-industry prototype to production lines. For example, we will need to assemble hundreds of similar satellites, rather than one or a few of a kind, as is now done. We will need to build thousands of mirrors, large and small. Finally, a production base may now exist (missile propellants, for example), but will require major expansion and/or modification to support anticipated future needs; such as producing thousands of terminal interceptors, rather than the 100-plus built for the old Sentinel/Safeguard system.

How will these new industries develop and old ones expand? They will certainly require planning and intelligent investment. While some argue that "the market" will provide the industry, the technological and political uncertainties of deployment coupled with the long lead times associated with many of the systems make it unlikely that "market forces" alone will provide sufficient incentive to overcome existing industrial problems. While many of the technologies will have civilian applications, the civilian applications will not be the sufficient drivers. The Department of Defense must invest in the physical plant, and in education of personnel, to ensure that the industrial base and skills are available when required.

Beginning the Transition

If it is still too early to estimate the overall dollar cost of developing and deploying a strategic defense—and I believe it is—it is not too early to identify the size and type of resources, in terms of personnel and facilities, required for proposed strategic defense architectures. We can begin by comparing resources related to alternative architectures. Such comparison provides knowledge of common resource requirements for all proposed defense alternatives, as well as additional requirements, associated with specific designs. Common resource requirements must be keyed to timelines. The additional architecture-specific requirements constitute trade-offs (as important as technical feasibility trade-offs) to be evaluated when considering which defense architecture to adopt.

Our security at the end of the transition period will depend critically on dealing with the scientific and industrial base issues. The ability of the scientific and industrial base to meet requirements must be judged in terms of manpower, facilities, and materials. These three particular factors deserve comment:

Manpower. Many observers have expressed concern over the effects of SDI on the scientific and industrial manpower base. Will all these resources be drawn off for SDI and leave too few for other military programs?

Scientific, engineering and technical (SET) manpower currently constitutes about 5 percent of the US labor force. In 1983, there were 1.5 million employed scientists, 1.9 million engineers, and approximately 1.6 million science and engineering technicians. The defense industrial base depends more on SET personnel than the civilian manufacturing sector (about 15 percent of the defense work force is employed in SET occupations, as compared to 3 percent in non-defense industry). However, recent studies show that the R&D phase of SDI will face manpower constraints only in selected areas (notably optics and artificial intelligence). The manpower situation during production and deployment phase is less certain and may depend on the speed of deployment. Mass production of high technology weapons may stress our current capabilities and draw labor away from other programs.

In the case of possible constraints in either the R&D or production phase, with proper policy decisions (establishing programs that develop people with the necessary skills, for example), many of these problem areas can probably be overcome. Also, allied manpower (Japan, Europe) can supplement our own resource base.

The United States may need a program to produce more SET personnel—a highly useful program no matter what becomes of SDI. With good planning and execution, manpower need not be a resource constraint.

Facilities. Key facilities in the R&D phase are largely government and industrial laboratories and test facilities. These appear to have sufficient capacity to support an expanded research program. Adequate test facilities may be more questionable, and additional test facilities may have to be built.

As with personnel, facility resources are less certain in a deployment phase. In some cases physical plants may have to be built and in other cases probably must be expanded. In either case it will take time and require national commitment to the SDI program. Facilities sufficiency will depend critically upon the architecture selected for SDI production, the time-phasing of the deployment, and our actual preparation.

Materials. Materials of interest range from raw materials to high technology manufactured materials. Will they be available in the time-frame of interest? These materials are critical to the production of new sensors, for optical and electronic applications. Further structural materials for use in space will also be essential. The question of whether "the market" is sufficient to assure the availability of new materials is a key one. I believe that new materials will not be available unless stimulated by government expenditures.

Summary

The key to supporting the transition to a strategic defense is not merely to identify what resource problems exist, but to identify subsequent solutions. This is a tall order in this early period. We are unsure what the future holds, we do not know what technologies might prove useful, and we can only speculate what our adversary may do. To meet these uncertainties we must develop plans and sufficiently flexible resource options that will allow us to support a defense deployment. It is this planning that must begin immediately if we are to maintain our security in the 21st century.

Jack H. Nunn is a Professor of Business and Administration at the Industrial College of the Armed Forces, National Defense University. Previously he was Acting Director, Mobilization Concepts Development Center, Institute for National Strategic Studies. Dr. Nunn is a graduate of the United States Military Academy and holds a Ph.D. from the Massachusetts Institute of Technology. He is a former Army officer with extensive overseas experience. He has published numerous articles on national security affairs and is the author of The Soviet First Strike Threat: The US Perspective *(New York: Praeger, 1982). In recent years he has conducted a number of studies on the US industrial base, resources acquisition, and technology for the Department of Defense.*

SDI AND THE FUTURE

David F. Emery

Predicting the political landscape of the future is an uncertain enterprise. Nevertheless, the reality is that today's policy decisions are key determinants of the future course of events. I will discuss the Strategic Defense Initiative (SDI) in this vein since the United States maintains that SDI can mean a safer and more stable future for the world.

President Reagan's Vision for the Future

A discussion of SDI and the future must necessarily begin with the goal set by the author of the initiative, President Ronald Reagan. In his speech of March 23, 1983, President Reagan envisioned a future in which our national security rested not upon the threat of nuclear retaliation, but on our ability to defend against potential attacks. He challenged us to determine whether, and if so how, advanced defensive technologies could make this vision possible.

The President's challenge in part responded to the changing nature of the military threat facing the United States while also recognizing the need to strengthen deterrence. For the past 20 years we have based our assumptions of mutual deterrence on the basic idea that if each side maintained roughly equal forces and equal capability to retaliate against attack, stability and deterrence would continue. Until recently, this concept of deterrence seemed not only sensible, but necessary, because we believed neither side could develop the defensive technology to effectively deter the other side.

Today, however, the situation is fundamentally different. Unfortunately, the Soviet Union has failed to show the hoped-for restraint in offensive and defensive forces which SALT seemed to promise. In addition, scientific developments and several emerging technologies now offer defense concepts that did not exist and could hardly have been conceived earlier. Defense breakthroughs have now progressed to the point where we can reasonably investigate whether new technologies give us the options to turn to defenses not only to enhance deterrence but to permit a more secure basis for deterrence.

SDI and Stability

One of our primary concerns is crisis stability, which implies a situation where no nation has an incentive to strike first in a serious crisis, nor to provoke a crisis that might lead to military confrontation. This situation exists only when the United States or Soviet Union cannot gain a significant advantage by initiating a conflict.

Both the United States and the Soviet Union recognize that a balanced offense/defense mix determines the strategic nuclear relationship. The Soviet Union must realize that a successful "creepout" or "breakout" in its own strategic defense capabilities (or conversely, unilateral restraint by the United States in this area) would shift the nuclear balance in its favor and potentially undermine the value of US and allied deterrent forces.

Through its ongoing overt and covert defense activities and its arms control policies, the Soviet Union has continually attempted to foster such a shift. In fact, the Soviet Union seeks to protect its gains in the strategic nuclear balance by limiting and delaying US defense programs, especially SDI. The Soviets are focusing on SDI because they are no longer alone in exploring the defensive potential of advanced technologies and because they may have to divert resources from proven ballistic missile programs to high-technology programs where we are likely to hold a competitive advantage.

To provide the desired security, advanced defensive technologies must be able to destroy enough of the attacking forces to deny an aggressor the ability to destroy significant portions of US targets. In a word, SDI must be militarily effective. The exact level of defense system capability required to achieve these ends can only be determined by evaluating the size, composition, effectiveness, and passive survivability of US forces relative to those of the Soviet Union.

An essential characteristic of a defense system is that it must be survivable—that is, able to maintain a sufficient degree of effectiveness to fulfill its mission, even in the face of determined attacks against it. In addition, a defensive system must not provide incentives to proliferate the ballistic missiles necessary to overcome it. Although existing ABM systems have lacked this essential capability, the newly emerging technologies under the SDI program have great potential in this regard. We must be concerned, therefore, with the degree to which our defensive systems encourage or discourage an adversary from overwhelming SDI with offensive systems and countermeasures. We must seek defensive options which clearly deter attempts to counter SDI with additional offensive forces. Finally, we must seek defensive options and an overall offensive/ defensive relationship with the Soviet Union that assures a stable transition from our current offensive posture to one more reliant on ballistic missile defense without diminishing the credibility of the US deterrent.

SDI and the Nuclear and Space Talks

At the nuclear and space talks in Geneva the United States has proposed a 10-year agreement not to deploy advanced strategic defenses and to conduct strategic defense research, development, and testing which are permitted by the ABM Treaty. Also, the United States has suggested that it and the Soviet Union eliminate all remaining ballistic missiles by 1996. To date, the Soviets have rejected this combined offer.

Instead, the Soviets insist that we agree to eliminate all strategic arms during that period, knowing full well that no alternative to nuclear deterrence presently exists. Eliminating nuclear weapons is a worthwhile goal, but it must be seen in the context of a time when we have, among other things, greater balance in conventional forces, an effective global ban on chemical and biological weapons, and insurance against Soviet noncompliance.

The Soviets are also trying to impose constraints more restrictive than those contained in the ABM Treaty. They talk of "strengthening" the ABM Treaty by redefining the activities permitted and prohibited under the treaty. We cannot accept such a proposal, especially given the Soviets' own active research, development, testing, and deployment program on strategic defenses. The Soviet terms would also prohibit much of the US strategic defense research now permitted by the ABM Treaty and would make future deployment so distant as to discourage active work on SDI. Fortunately, the President intends to pursue a vigorous SDI research effort as permitted by the ABM Treaty, both as an investment in, and insurance for, a safer and more stable strategic balance.

Before the October 1986 Reykjavik meeting between President Reagan and Soviet General Secretary Gorbachev, the United States had repeatedly made clear its parallel commitments to the SDI program and to continued adherence to the ABM Treaty. In a letter to Soviet General Secretary Gorbachev, President Reagan stated that, if both sides can agree on radical reductions in strategic offensive weapons, the United States would be prepared to sign an agreement containing the following guidelines. First, through 1991, both sides would agree to confine themselves to research, development, and testing, permitted by the ABM Treaty, to determine whether advanced systems of strategic defense are technically feasible. Second, after 1991, a new treaty would specify that if either side should decide to deploy such a system, that side must offer a plan (negotiated over a two-year period) for sharing the benefits of strategic defense and for eliminating offensive ballistic missiles. Third, if after two years of negotiation, the two sides could not agree, either side would be free to deploy an advanced strategic defensive system after giving six months' notice to the other.

At Reykjavik, President Reagan and General Secretary Gorbachev almost reached a common ground on a time period during which both sides would agree not to withdraw from the ABM Treaty in order to deploy advanced strategic defenses. Gorbachev insisted on a 10-year period; the President was prepared to agree to that, provided we could agree with the Soviets on three issues: the regime of control over defenses, a program for reducing offensive ballistic missiles, and expectations on what each side could do after the 10 years expired.

On the regime of control over defenses, President Reagan proposed to Gorbachev that both sides strictly abide by the limitations of the ABM Treaty. Gorbachev insisted on what he called measures to "strengthen" the ABM Treaty but these measures, in fact, amounted to an attempt to amend it. Specifically, he proposed to restrict to the laboratory testing of all space elements or components of antiballistic missile defense.

With regard to offensive reductions, the United States proposed eliminating all ballistic missiles remaining after 1991 during a second five-year phase ending in 1996. The Soviets, on the other hand, called for eliminating all remaining strategic offensive weapons during that period.

As for each side's rights after 10 years, the United States proposed that either side should be free to deploy defense unless the parties agree otherwise. The

Soviets proposed to enter into a new negotiation after 10 years on all issues related to the ABM Treaty.

We should continue to discuss with the Soviets our view of what the ABM Treaty permits. They must understand, however, that we do not wish to create limits more stringent than those already incorporated in the treaty and, indeed, see Soviet efforts to do so as but thinly veiled efforts to inhibit SDI.

The United States believes that, by the early 1990s, both sides at Geneva should seek to achieve the deep reductions in strategic and intermediate-range nuclear forces that were discussed at Reykjavik. If so, stability at substantially lower levels would occur, by reducing the most threatening systems and encouraging force structures that make preemptive attack much less likely. While these reductions were taking place, SDI research would continue, thus providing future strategic defense options while maintaining strong incentives for further reducing offensive nuclear forces.

Subsequently, with all ballistic missiles eliminated, the United States would not face a Soviet first-strike capability, yet would retain aircraft and cruise missiles to maintain deterrence. Strategic defenses would serve both the United States and the Soviet Union as an insurance policy which would prevent cheating or the use of ballistic missiles by third countries.

However, our approach toward such a future strategic relationship must recognize a continuing need to rely on nuclear deterrence well into the future. Any transition toward less reliance on nuclear weapons must be carefully conceived, carefully coordinated with Congress and our allies, and carefully phased in to ensure stability along the way.

The Need for Strategic Defenses

If we were to couple elimination of ballistic missiles with deployment of strategic defenses as our proposal envisions, we would have a critical hedge against cheating. We would also deter it, since, with ever-growing effective defenses, ballistic missiles would gradually lose the overwhelming military value they now have. If defenses exist to stop ballistic missiles, then there would obviously be few military reasons for bringing them back. Strategic defenses would thus provide a complete insurance policy for arms control.

The President's proposal envisions a world where the most menacing weapons, ballistic missiles, have been eliminated by arms control and simultaneously rendered obsolete by defenses. What we agree to however, must be backed up with physical guarantees.

President Reagan's offer suggests that strategic defense can assist and strengthen arms control. In fact, strategic defense technologies represent the most promising way to reduce the risk of nuclear war since the space launches made the reconnaissance satellite possible. SDI could prove an even more radical advance than the emergence of "national technical means" of verification.

The President has proposed showing the Soviets how defenses and arms control can work together, on a scale few people have dreamed of. Finally, his proposed idea can allay Soviet fears that we are seeking a first-strike capability through SDI. If ballistic missiles are phased out, a first-strike will become impossible. The swift sword of today will become the defensive shield of the future.

The Contributions of Strategic Defenses

Strategic defense, once deployed by both sides, can make three contributions to mutual security. First, it can enhance stability by complicating any surprise attack, thus making a preemptive attack extremely difficult to plan, much less execute, with confidence. Second, it can counteract nuclear blackmail by blunting the missile threat. Third, by making ballistic missiles less effective, defenses can help create military balance and improve world politics. It was SDI that brought the Soviets back to the bargaining table in Geneva after their 1983 walk-out from the arms control talks. Any measures we can take to eliminate the offensive ballistic missile threat are measures we should pursue.

In short, defensive research points toward a world in which ballistic missiles play a reduced role, in which fast, first-strike systems will become much less effective, and in which slower, second-strike systems will domi-nate the military equation. SDI is a way of removing the current hair-trigger balance based on the primacy of bal-listic missiles. All these advantages are precisely the goals we have sought to achieve with arms control over the years.

Any future US decision to deploy defensive systems would, of course, lead to an important change in the structure of US and Soviet forces. We must continue to examine ways of managing offense/defense relation-ships to achieve a more stable balance through strategic arms control. Above all, we must seek to ensure that the mix of offensive and defensive forces removes first-strike options from both sides.

The United States does not view defensive measures as a way of establishing military superiority. Because we have no ambitions in this regard, deployments of SDI must occur in the context of a cooperative, equitable, and verifiable arms control environment that regulates the offensive and defensive developments and deployments of the United States and the Soviet Union. Such an environment is most nec-essary during the transition period from deterrence based on a nuclear retaliation, through deterrence based on a balance of offensive and defensive forces, to the period when advanced defensive systems are fully deployed. Throughout the transition, arms control agreements could help manage and establish guidelines for deploying defensive systems.

Looking Ahead

When we embarked on our SDI research, President Reagan stated that this program would fully comply with our treaty obligations. From its inception, he directed that this program be planned to meet that commitment—and we have done so. In October 1985, the United States completed an extensive review of the ABM Treaty and the associated negotiating record which led President Reagan to conclude that we needed a broader interpretation of our authority. Since October 1985, we have continued to review all records and data on this subject. Based on the review, I see the President's broader interpretation of the ABM Treaty as fully justified and workable.

Our technical understanding of the feasibility of providing advanced defensive options—options which could meet our more expansive criteria—is growing rapidly. The costs of continuing our current restrictive policy regarding the SDI program—in terms of additional resources, time, and increased technical uncertainty—are growing correspondingly. As a result, the balance is shifting between the price that the United States and its allies must pay for an SDI program structured within the bounds of the more restrictive ABM Treaty view and our overall security requirements.

Technological advances inevitably have profound military and political effects. Statesmanship must not ignore the advance of technology, but must look ahead to study the promise and potential pitfalls of these advances, especially as they affect international security. SDI is designed to match such technology with the statesman's willingness to discuss such technology at the arms control table.

David F. Emery was Deputy Director, US Arms Control and Disarmament Agency, from 1983 to 1988. Representing the 1st Congressional District of Maine between 1975 and 1983, Mr. Emery served on the House Armed Service Committee from 1977 to 1983. Between 1971 and 1975, Mr. Emery served in the Maine State Legislature. Mr. Emery holds a B.S. degree in Electronic Engineering from Worchester Polytechnic Institute.

PART III

ALLIANCE IMPLICATIONS

IMPLICATIONS OF SDI FOR US RELATIONS WITH NATO ALLIES

Arthur F. Burns and Roger P. Labrie

President Reagan explicitly included America's allies in the defensive umbrella against ballistic missile attack when he unveiled the Strategic Defense Initiative (SDI) in March 1983. Initial reactions from West European capitals, nevertheless, were largely skeptical.[1] The President's commitment in that March speech to maintain "a solid capability for flexible response,"[2] while SDI research began, acknowledged the continued reliance of our allies on US strategic offensive forces to deter a Soviet attack. Such assurance, however, did little to assuage European concerns.

Many of the European fears about SDI are similar to those articulated in the late 1960s when both superpowers were pursuing proposed anti-ballistic missile (ABM) defenses. These concerns relate to the impact of missile defenses on US-Soviet nuclear arms competition, East-West political relations and the prospects for arms control, NATO's military strategy of flexible response, American security guarantees to Western Europe, and the credibility of independent British and French nuclear deterrents.

Our European allies applauded the 1972 ABM Treaty because it seemed to alleviate their concerns about ballistic missile defenses. Those concerns, however, resurfaced in the wake of President Reagan's speech on SDI. Our allies regret the absence of consultations between Washington and allied capitals prior to President Reagan's speech. Furthermore, the Reagan SDI speech coincided with allied debates over deployment of Pershing IIs and ground-launched cruise missiles. Because the President did not clarify that SDI was a prudent response to the Soviet Union's longstanding efforts to develop advanced ballistic missile defenses, our allies interpreted Reagan's remarks as an American effort to achieve strategic superiority. Moreover, many

157

Europeans were undoubtedly startled by the President's announced goal of rendering nuclear weapons—the ultimate deterrent to Soviet aggression—impotent and obsolete. Subsequent statements by administration officials added confusion to the early debate on SDI by failing to distinguish clearly between SDI's near-term and longer-run objectives. As a result, some critics took the President's objective to mean that the United States was "giving up nuclear deterrence and moving toward a different strategic world, beyond deterrence."[3]

True, West Europeans have become more supportive of SDI in recent months because they now better understand the program's objectives. The allies now recognize that SDI is no mere unilateral effort on the part of the United States. Europeans know, too, that the Soviet Union has long been pursuing its own version of SDI. The Soviet Union, for instance, maintains around Moscow the world's only operational ABM system and is currently upgrading and expanding that system to the limits permitted by the ABM Treaty. Also, construction of a new ballistic missile detection and tracking radar in Krasnoyarsk, Siberia, clearly suggests a more extensive ballistic missile defense deployment. Furthermore, Soviet research on advanced technologies for missile defense (including space weapons) indicates that Soviet leaders have a more vigorous concept of deterrence than the one most Western nations thought was enshrined in the ABM Treaty.[4]

Another reason for increased allied support of SDI is the extensive consultation that has recently been taking place between Washington and allied capitals. In particular, the US has invited our allies to participate in the SDI research program, thus opening an important avenue for sharing information and fostering understanding of the issues surrounding SDI.

Still, the basis for sustained allied support of SDI is not as firm as it needs to be. Stronger allied support dictates closer agreement within the alliance on the strategic and political implications of SDI as well as larger involvement of our allies in the actual SDI program.

In fact, SDI raises difficult questions for the Western Alliance. Many Europeans still think that ballistic missile defense may undermine the traditional strategic foundation of Western security—namely, deterrence of Soviet aggression by the threat of retaliation with offensive nuclear weapons. They argue that deploying ballistic missile defenses extensively could diminish the mutual vulnerability of the superpowers—the heart, in European eyes, of the deterrence concept. Since neither superpower will likely be able to deploy a perfect defense of both its homeland and those of its allies, the very imperfection of anti-missile defenses could encourage a build-up of offensive nuclear arsenals to overwhelm the adversary's defenses. Europeans fear that such a development would also intensify competition in defensive weapons, doom arms control, heighten superpower concerns about the first-strike potential of the other side, and thus exacerbate East-West tensions.[5] Some SDI critics view the apparent lack of progress in the current arms talks in Geneva as resulting from the American inclination to develop extensive ballistic missile defenses.

Of most immediate concern to our European allies are the potential implications of ballistic missile defenses for NATO's strategy of flexible response. That strategy was formulated in the mid-1960s to react to growing Soviet intercontinental nuclear forces which created a serious danger for the United States and cast doubt on the credibility of its "massive retaliation" doctrine. The current strategy of flexible response requires that NATO maintain forces capable of responding to varied levels of Soviet aggression. Should such response prove inadequate, the allies would escalate the conflict to higher levels to convince the aggressor to cease his attack and withdraw from captured territory.[6]

The current strategy of flexible response presumes a rough equivalence of shared risks between the United States and its NATO allies. Should deterrence fail and armed aggression occur against NATO territory, the presence of American forces in Europe practically assures US involvement in the conflict from the start. NATO's flexible response strategy and its threat of escalating the conflict up to the strategic nuclear level implies that the American homeland faces risks comparable to those of its European allies. Some Europeans fear that the common risks which now bind the alliance together could sharply diverge if the superpowers deployed ballistic missile defenses. In that event, the risks facing the United States would be smaller than those confronting its allies. In the extreme case, Soviet ballistic missile defenses could neutralize the US strategic nuclear deterrent, thereby drastically lessening Soviet risks in attacking Western Europe. Europeans fear that if such a conflict escalates to the nuclear level, the superpowers might find it expedient to confine their nuclear exchanges to the European continent. On this line of reasoning, even if our European allies had comparable defenses against a ballistic missile attack, Western Europe would still remain vulnerable to superior Soviet/Warsaw Pact conventional forces and to other means of nuclear attack—that is, cruise missiles, fighter-bombers, and nuclear artillery. Thus, some Europeans fear that SDI—if matched by a comparable Soviet deployment—could weaken deterrence and undercut NATO unity.[7]

Western Europeans are now concerned that the enormous cost of SDI may weaken NATO's other defense capabilities. Funds to support it might be diverted from US research or procurement programs for conventional military forces of special relevance to Western Europe. This possibility is especially worrisome to those who believe that mutual superpower deployment of ballistic missile defenses will increase the risk of conventional war in Europe. Moreover, the defense budget in Western Europe, even now inadequate for a dependable conventional defense, could be strained further if our allies had to support a European version of SDI.[8]

One final strategic concern of our allies is the potential impact of ballistic missile defenses on the viability and credibility of the British and French nuclear deterrents. Since both countries have only a relatively small number of ballistic missiles, an expansion of Soviet ballistic missile defenses would diminish their retaliatory ability, especially if those defenses protected major cities. Until now, the ABM Treaty has provided some assurance of British and French ability to retaliate, but that assurance could hardly survive an extensive Soviet anti-missile defense. The nullifying effect of superpower deployment of ballistic missile defenses concerns not only these two allies but also other Europeans who consider the independent British and French nuclear forces a prudent backup to the American nuclear umbrella in Western Europe.[9]

Much of the early SDI debate within the Alliance addressed strategic implications of the superpowers' widespread ballistic missile defenses by the superpowers; the scope of the debate has now broadened because our allies have been invited to participate in the SDI research program. The United States issued this invitation for several reasons. First, because SDI research seeks to determine the technical feasibility of defending all NATO countries against ballistic missile attack, our allies should have the opportunity to participate in the program. Second, mutual participation will help continue the West's technological and economic leadership. Third, allied involvement in the research phase of SDI will undoubtedly lead to broad support for the program in Europe.

However, some European critics still view initial SDI research as an economic threat. They believe that most SDI research will result in technologies applicable to space exploration, as well as to high-powered computers, artificial intelligence, and other civilian commercial uses. Consequently, some European experts fear that a massive infusion of government funds into research and development in the United States could widen the gap in high technology that already exists between the United States and Western Europe.[10]

Besides their political and strategic reservations about SDI, some of our allies question the economic benefits they would derive from participating in the program. Would they receive a significant share of the research contracts? Would the contracts involve work on leading-edge technologies that can benefit allied competition in world markets? Would SDI research draw Europe's best minds away from work that is more directly beneficial to commerce? Would US security restrictions on the results of European research limit their application to civilian sectors of European economies? According to press accounts, these questions were key ones raised in the negotiations with London and Bonn on participation in SDI research.[11] What is more, we must evaluate how the so-called framework agreements that emerged from those talks will actually work out in practice.

So far, only Britain, West Germany, and Israel have accepted the US offer to participate in SDI research by signing a memorandum of understanding (or framework agreement). The United States expects a similar agreement with Italy. Other allied governments—notably Canada, France, Denmark, Norway, the Netherlands, and Japan—have so far refrained from formal involvement in SDI research but will not prevent their business firms or research institutes from seeking SDI contracts.

At present, the results of SDI research are hopeful but inconclusive—and so they will remain for the immediate future. However, if the SDI research program shows that significant ballistic missile defenses for the United States and its allies are technically feasible, the Alliance will face a fateful decision. A decision not to deploy could be disastrous, particularly if the Soviets in the meantime have a technological breakthrough and proceed to deploy their counterpart to SDI. In such a world, the Soviets could neutralize the US strategic nuclear deterrent—as well as those of Britain and France. In fact, under cover of such an umbrella, Moscow might be bold enough to contemplate aggression, using the superior conventional forces of the Warsaw Pact. In any case, the pressures on our allies to seek accommodation with the Soviet Union would quickly become overwhelming.

A key question arises. As leader of the Alliance, how could the United States ease the transition from an offensive strategic environment to one dominated by defensive weapons, if such a transition were deemed necessary? Regrettably, at present there may be no responsible answer to this frightfully difficult question. But there are some procedural principles that we need to follow.

First, the United States must continue the pattern of close consultation with its allies on security issues established with regard to Intermediate-range Nuclear Force (INF) deployments and SDI. Such consultations have already resulted in better understanding about SDI research. In particular, President Reagan's December 1984 meeting with Prime Minister Thatcher produced common understanding on the following points: (1) the purpose of SDI is to maintain a military balance with the Soviet Union, not to achieve superiority; (2) in view of existing treaty obligations, actual deployment of SDI will depend on negotiations; (3) the basic aim of SDI is to enhance deterrence, not to undermine it; and (4) East-West negotiations should aim to achieve security with reduced levels of offensive systems on both sides.[12]

Given the diverse interests and strategic concerns of our European allies, consultations between Washington and Europe must explore the reasons for possible SDI deployment, the criteria for decisionmaking, the role of SDI in arms control, and how deployment would eventually take place. Regarding the last point, suffice it to say that whatever level of defense proves feasible under SDI, it will have to provide equal levels of protection for the United States and NATO at each stage of deployment. Otherwise, the bond of shared risks holding the Alliance together will break, with tragic consequences for the West.

Another step for promoting consensus within the Alliance is encouraging the greatest attainable level of allied involvement in SDI research. The more familiar our allies become with SDI's technical capabilities, the better decisions they can make regarding movement to subsequent states in the program's evolution. In particular, the allies must be confident about whatever decisions they make regarding the testing and deployment stages.

We should bear in mind, however, that involving our allies in SDI inevitably leads to some controversy over the economic and security issues surrounding work contracts. Likewise, the US should remain circumspect in judging the Eureka program and proposals for an exclusive European Defense Initiative.[13] Rather than competing with SDI, the programs must be complementary and reinforce one another. As things presently stand, Britain and West Germany will participate in both Eureka and SDI.

Of vital importance, too, is that we continue to strive to agree on arms control in Geneva. In fact, reductions in the levels of strategic and intermediate-range nuclear forces will help determine the level of protection SDI can provide to the West. Moreover, any move beyond the research stage of SDI may require us to eliminate the current disparity in conventional forces and chemical weaponry in Central Europe.

Since we are presently far from certain that we can achieve the arms control prerequisites for SDI deployment and Alliance harmony, the United States might consider a new set of mutual and verifiable restrictions on the testing and deployment of advanced ballistic missile defense systems. In return, both sides would substantially reduce their offensive ballistic missiles.

In view of the enormous uncertainties about deploying extensive defenses against ballistic missiles, the United States and NATO should explore feasible alternatives to extensive ballistic missile defenses—even as we proceed to intensify research on SDI with the help of our allies. There is no simple or obvious path to a more stable strategic and political environment in this dangerous world. Thus, we must continue working toward this objective with the Soviets in Geneva and with our European allies in every NATO capital.

Arthur F. Burns, 1904-1987, was US Ambassador to the Federal Republic of Germany (1981-85) and Distinguished Scholar-in-Residence, American Enterprise Institute, 1978-81; 1985-87). Dr. Burns held many positions in government and in the academic world. He served on the President's Council of Economic Advisors, 1953-56 and as Chairman of the Federal Reserve Board, 1970-78. In addition, he taught economics at Rutgers University, 1927-44 and Columbia University, 1944-58. Dr. Burns has published extensively and is most known for Measuring Business Cycles (with W.C. Mitchell) (1946), The Defense Sector and the American Economy (1968), and Reflections of an Economic Policy Maker (1979).

Roger P. Labrie is a defense consultant who was Research Associate at the American Enterprise Institute. Among his many publications are (with Robert J. Pranger), Nuclear Strategy and National Security: Points of View (Washington, DC: AEI, 1977) and SALT Handbook: Key Documents and Issues, 1972-1979 (Washington, DC: AEI, 1979). Mr. Labrie holds a B.A. from St. Anselms, an M.A. from Georgetown University, and is a Ph.D. Candidate at Columbia University.

NOTES

1. See David S. Yost, "European Anxieties about Ballistic Missile Defense," *Washington Quarterly,* Vol. 7, No. 4 (Fall 1984), pp. 112-113; and John Newhouse, "The Diplomatic Round," *New Yorker,* July 22, 1985, pp. 37-54.

2. Appendix A, "Text of Address by the President to the Nation," in Paul E. Gallis, Mark M. Lowenthal, and Marcia S. Smith, *The Strategic Defense Initiative and United States Alliance Strategy* (Washington, D.C.: Library of Congress, Congressional Research Service, Report No. 85-48F, 1 February 1985), pp. 74-75.

3. See, for example, Pierre Lellouche, "SDI and The Atlantic Alliance," *SAIS Review,* Vol. 5, No. 2 (Summer-Fall 1985), p. 68.

4. See *Soviet Strategic Defense Programs* (Washington, D.C.: Department of Defense and Department of State, October 1985).

5. For instance, see Lellouche, "SDI and The Atlantic Alliance"; Christoph Bertram, "Strategic Defense and the Western Alliance," *Daedalus,* "Weapons in Space, Vol. II: Implications for Security," Vol. 114, No. 3 (Summer 1985); and Yost, "European Anxieties about Ballistic Missile Defense."

6. See James R. Schlesinger, "The Theater Nuclear Force Posture in Europe," A Report to the U.S. Congress, April 1975, in Robert J. Pranger and Roger P. Labrie (eds.), *Nuclear Strategy and National Security* (Washington, D.C.: American Enterprise Institute, 1977), p. 171. For an overview of the Evolution of NATO strategy, see J. Michael Legge, *Theater Nuclear Weapons and the NATO Strategy of Flexible Response* (Santa Monica, CA: Rand Corporation, R-2964-FF, April 1983), pp. 2-10; and David N. Schwartz, *NATO's Nuclear Dilemmas* (Washington, D.C.: Brookings Institution, 1983), Chapter 6.

7. See Yost, "European Anxieties about Ballistic Missile Defense," p. 122: Bertram, "Strategic Defense and the Western Alliance," pp. 291-294; and Fen Osler Hampson, "Escalation in Europe," in Graham T. Allison, Albert Carnesale, and Joseph S. Nye, Jr., (eds.), *Hawks, Doves, and Owls: An Agenda for Avoiding Nuclear War* (New York: W.W. Norton & Co., 1985), pp. 89-90.

8. See Thierry De Montbrial, "The European Dimension," *Foreign Affairs*, "American and the World 1985," Vol. 64, No. 3 (1986), p. 508; *Strategic Survey 1984-1985*, (London International Institute for Strategic Studies, 1985), pp. 12-13, 16; Lellouche, "SDI and The Atlantic Alliance," p. 80; and Bertram, "Strategic Defense and the Western Alliance," p. 288.

9. See Lellouche, "SDI and the Atlantic Alliance," pp. 71 and 76; Yost, "European Anxieties about Ballistic Missile Defense," pp. 125-127; David S. Yost, "France's Deterrent Posture and Security in Europe, Part I: Capabilities and Doctrine," *Adelphi Papers*, No. 194 (Winter 1984/85), pp. 25-26; and Bertram, "Strategic Defense and The Western Alliance," pp. 285-286.

10. For example, see Lellouche, "SDI and The Atlantic Alliance," pp. 79-80. On the widening "high-tech gap" between Europe and the United States, see "Europe's High-Tech Gap Sets Off Warning Bells," *U.S. News and World Report*, May 27, 1985, pp. 45-46.

11. David Dickson, "British Cabinet Split on SDI Agreement," *Science*, December 13, 1985, p. 1252; Karen DeYoung, "Britain Joins U.S. in SDI Research," *Washington Post*, December 7, 1985; and Frederick Kempe, "Germans Debate an Accord on Star Wars," *Wall Street Journal*, 21 March 1986.

12. *The Strategic Defense Initiative*, Special Report No. 129 (Washington, D.C.: Department of State, June 1985), p. 5.

13. See, for example, Manfred Woerner, "A Missile Defense for NATO Europe," *Strategic Review*, Vol. 14, No. 1 (Winter 1986).

IMPLICATIONS OF SDI FOR NATO'S CONVENTIONAL FORCE POSTURE

Franz-Joseph Schulze

The implications of the Strategic Defense Initiative (SDI) for the Atlantic Alliance, its strategy to deter and prevent war, and the resultant conclusions about force planning will largely depend on the outcome of research efforts made by both sides—the United States of America and the Soviet Union. What technologies will be available to whom and at what time? How efficient will the defensive systems be? How will both conventional and nuclear potentials evolve in the meantime? Consequently, the implications of anti-missile defense systems for the strategies of either side will continue to be conditional for some time to come.

We may proceed from the assumption that most of the technological breakthroughs necessary to make SDI effective are likely to strengthen the Alliance's conventional defense posture during the next 20 years. We should not assess the implications of SDI, therefore, assuming SDI will be implemented at a specific point in time in the next century. On the contrary, we must primarily address the problems of transition, especially as far as the conventional defense in Europe is concerned.

Changing Parameters

Deterrence and Defense. The primary objective of the North Atlantic Alliance is to prevent war through deterrence—to prevent any war, a conventional as well as a nuclear war.

Deterrence means making it evident to a potential aggressor that neither military force nor intimidation by blatantly demonstrating superior military power holds any promise of success. Deterrence implies balanced, sufficiently strong, and immediately available forces—and the defender's capability to choose among conventional, tactical nuclear, and strategic nuclear forces to confront the attacker with an incalculable risk. Close, indivisible ties between Western Europe and the United States are the only means to ensure a balance of forces adequate to cause the potential aggressor to adopt a course of rational political conduct.

The Perception of Deterrence in the Strategic Nuclear and Conventional Sphere. The perception of deterrence depends on a rather strange dichotomy of conventional and strategic-nuclear components. In the conventional sphere, deterrence is credible only if backed by a visible and unquestionable resolve to fight and defend. Deterrence rests upon the ability to deny the aggressor his objectives. Effective deterrence does not necessarily mean a watertight defense capability. In the conventional sphere, even a defense capability which is not "gapless" or 100 percent effective will deter the potential aggressor, provided such defense can disrupt the overall cohesion of his offensive operations and deny him the swift seizure of strategically important objectives.

By contrast, in the strategic nuclear sphere, deterrence depends primarily on the capability of destroying the aggressor through retaliation, indeed of launching such a retaliatory strike even after one's own forces have received the first strike. Succinctly put, "an assured second-strike capability is decisive for strategic stability, since it denies the adversary the ability to launch a first strike."[1]

The causes of this dichotomy in the perception of deterrence are obvious. In the conventional sphere, successful defense has always been conceivable, provided the necessary resources are available; effective defense against intercontinental ballistic missiles, on the other hand, seems to defy the limits of the art. If, however, technological developments make an effective defense possible—even against ballistic missiles—then we should question whether we must continue to define nuclear deterrence in terms different from those applied in the conventional sphere. Must strategic nuclear deterrence still be based solely on the assured capability to destroy the aggressor? Or will it also become true in the strategic nuclear sphere—even more so than in the conventional one—that to deter the aggressor, we can deny him quick achievement of his strategic objective?

Reducing the Threat of a First-Strike Capability. An aggressor who plans to disarm his adversary by a nuclear first strike must be absolutely certain of his success, since even a partial failure threatens him with immediate annihilation during a retaliatory strike. No watertight defense system is necessary to deny him this certainty. Even an imperfect strategic defense posture will deprive the aggressor of the required certainty and discourage temptations to launch a nuclear first strike. Undoubtedly, an aggressor who knows most of his strategic weapons will not reach their target (with the surviving targets to include perhaps those most important to his adversary's nuclear capabilities) will not undertake a nuclear first strike. Consequently, deploying a strategic defense system would reduce the threat of a first strike. Reducing such a nuclear first-strike capability, however, is a decisive contribution to a more secure world and to greater stability.

New Chances for Arms Control Policy. To date, Western attempts have not secured the necessary strategic nuclear balance at a lower level through arms control agreements—agreements that were probably bound to fail based on the mutual assured destruction (MAD) concept. The need to secure, at all costs, the capability to destroy the aggressor in retaliation involves the tendency—on both sides—to continually expand the quantity and quality of nuclear weapons.

Thus far, no arms control agreement has ever changed this tendency. On the contrary, by permitting high ceilings for strategic nuclear weapon systems, these agreements have perpetuated the basic structure of today's nuclear postures. MAD continues to be the foundation of deterrence. Until now, arms control agreements have permitted an increase of Soviet forces, both in size and in effectiveness, to the point where US land-based offensive forces and their accompanying command and control have become seriously vulnerable.[2]

The argument that a strategic defense system which is not absolutely impenetrable will literally provoke the aggressor to increase his offensive potentials fails to recognize a very important criterion. From the beginning of the SDI debate, the United States has stated that a strategic defense system must be "cost-effective" (e.g., that building up the defenses must be cheaper than expanding the offensive potential). Hence, no cost incentive exists to increase the number of offensive missiles. Paul Nitze talked of the "favorable marginal cost" of the defense systems.[3] If multiplying the offensive weapons is, therefore, not a logical response to the buildup of the strategic defense system, then both sides have an incentive to cut down the offensive potentials.

Soviet Defense Initiative. The Soviet Union has never adopted the concept of "Mutual Assured Destruction" since it presupposes accepting one's own vulnerability. On the contrary, Soviet strategic thinking has always greatly emphasized damage limitation through passive protection (such as evacuation and shelters) and active defense.

Consequently, the Soviet Union began developing and deploying anti-missile defense systems around Moscow long ago. The Soviets have had ample opportunity for rigorous live testing under realistic conditions and for gaining practical experience in operating these systems. In fact, the Soviet Union is the only nation which currently has an anti-missile system in operation—a system which the Soviets take great pains to continually improve and modernize.[4] Even those who feel relieved that, thanks to President Reagan's initiative, the United States may soon overtake the Soviet Union in the research of relevant technologies, cannot deny that the Soviet Union is considerably ahead of the United States in applying such technologies and in improving anti-missile defense systems.

At the same time, the Soviet Union's air defense system covers wide areas and is second to none in terms of its deployment density. Elements of this air defense system have repeatedly been tested for their suitability as an anti-missile system. The SAM-5, for example, has been launched about 50 times against ballistic missiles. While such anti-missile capability is currently marginal, the Soviet Union may develop a respectable anti-missile capability, particularly against short- and intermediate-range missiles, using the SAM-10 and the SAM-X-12, which are still undergoing tests. The US Department of Defense believes that the SAM-X-12 may be capable of intercepting ballistic missiles such as LANCE, Pershing I, and Pershing II.[5]

Gradual Reorientation of the Strategic Concept. Intensive research on the options for the buildup of a strategic defense is in full swing on both sides and it cannot be banned. The deployment of strategic defense systems, and especially the expansion of Soviet air defense to include an "ATBM" capability (e.g., the ability to ward off so-called "tactical" ballistic missiles) would gravely affect Europe's security. NATO must adapt its strategic concept and its force structures to these changing threat parameters—and it must do so quickly, even though the necessary measures can only take place on a step-by-step basis.

In the foreseeable future SDI will not totally replace the concept of Mutual Assured Destruction. The capability of destroying the aggressor through retaliation may continue as the primary nuclear doctrine for a long time. The question is whether a defensive addition in the strategic nuclear area might not help us to reduce gradually—and, hopefully, reduce increasingly—our current dependence on this ultimate means of deterrence. Will the integration of defensive components make deterrence more secure? Toward this end, a perfect, impenetrable defense is *not* necessary. Assured "strategic invulnerability" will remain a distant vision for the foreseeable future—and it may well be an unattainable goal. Hence, idealistic speculations about conflict scenarios which proceed from a notion of invulnerability of the top superpowers are, therefore, unrealistic. By the same token, we should not argue that an imperfect strategic defense system is pointless. The alternative confronting us is *not* "all or nothing" (e.g., either an impenetrable defense system or none at all).

Any meaningful discussion of the implications of SDI for the strategy of NATO hinges on what former Secretary of Defense Weinberger called the "options of transition,"[6] options that might well be available in a comparatively short time.

The Need to Strengthen Conventional Defense

The NATO Territory as a Strategic Entity. Any defense initiative which truly claims to be "strategic" must include the European theater. Alliance cohesion is based on the principle that the NATO territory constitutes a single strategic entity.

To the West Europeans, the Warsaw Pact's conventional superiority—which is longstanding and has grown continually in recent years—has a strategic quality. In West European eyes, the Soviet short- and intermediate-range missiles (SRINF and INF)—from the SS-20s through the SS-23s—are not "tactical nuclear weapons" but strategic weapons. The strategic nature of forces and weapons systems does not depend on their range, accuracy, or destructive power, but on the political objectives such weapons support.

The threat to Europe has a strategic quality for the United States of America as well. The combined capabilities of the European states, confronted by the

Soviet Union's nuclear weapons are insufficient to deter the threat or use of force. No matter how we read East-West comparisons of population figures, economic capabilities, and military potentials, a brief look at the map and the geostrategic pattern of Europe quickly demonstrates that the security of Western Europe depends primarily on a close Alliance with the United States. Conversely, the status of the United States as a world power would quickly diminish if Europe should fall under Soviet influence, either as a result of Soviet military aggression or of European accommodation due to mutual loss of confidence in NATO. Hence, strengthening our capabilities to counter the Warsaw Pact's conventional superiority and the Soviet short- and intermediate-range missile threat is an urgent priority for *all* NATO members.

Conventional Superiority of the Warsaw Pact. As pointed out, the Warsaw Pact has always enjoyed superiority in conventional forces, and it has expanded that superiority through continued improvements in both the quantity and quality of its forces. Its relentless arms buildup in every field since the mid-1960s has strengthened the Pact's offensive character—and given it the element of surprise.[7] In addition, the Soviet Union has geared its military posture to restricting NATO's possible responses, thereby depriving NATO of its core element—flexibility. Not only is the Soviet Union gaining new options for its military strategy, but by limiting NATO's margin of responses, the Soviets are realizing new ways of attaining their political objectives.

The North Atlantic Alliance must be able to implement its strategy, and stronger conventional forces are the prerequisite to flexible response. In fact, improvements at the conventional level are more urgent than they have ever been before. A widespread consensus exists in NATO on this very question, as proven by a whole series of special Alliance efforts to improve its conventional capabilities: "Allied Defenses in the Seventies (AD 70s)," "Rapid Reinforcement Program Europe

(RRP)," "Short Term Defense Program (STDP)," "Long Term Defense Program (LTDP)," and "Follow-on Forces Attack (FOFA)." However, General Bernard Rogers, the former Supreme Allied Commander Europe, could only conclude that "although Allied Command Europe is getting stronger every year the gap between the conventional capabilities of NATO and those of the Warsaw Pact gets wider each year."[8] He has repeatedly warned the nations that "the Alliance's conventional capabilities today are clearly inadequate to meet the growing Warsaw Pact conventional threat" and that "this inadequacy might place us in a position where for our defense we would have to rely on a possibly very early use of nuclear weapons."[9]

The continuation of the decade-old debate on the causes of the imbalances and gaps in NATO's force triad is futile and poisons the political climate. NATO cannot continue to complain about the unwillingness on the part of all allies to pay the price of a balanced, effective defense capability; the ready acceptance of the "cheap approach" of basing deterrence primarily on nuclear weapons; the alleged calculation of the Europeans that by exercising restraint in the buildup of conventional capabilities they can ensure an American nuclear response even in case of a purely conventional attack by the Warsaw Pact.

Ever since the Lisbon Force Goals of February 1952, NATO members have known that to establish a conventional balance between NATO and Warsaw Pact one would be faced with insurmountable obstacles, not only in the financial, but also in the political field. The cost to the West of such a conventional arms buildup would dramatically exceed present defense budgets. The United States and the United Kingdom would have to reintroduce the draft and the European countries would have to extend their periods of military service. Owing to the need for a larger number of in-place forces, the Federal Republic of Germany would, in effect, become a huge military fortress for an indefinite period of time.

Finally, the downward demographic trend in all the member nations makes any notion of a potential numerical growth in armed forces a fantasy.

However, for NATO's conventional defense to be effective, it is not necessary to achieve perfect equilibrium. The point is not to match the Warsaw Pact in terms of divisions, tanks, aircraft, and ships. What the Alliance needs is the conventional capability to hinder the aggressor from effectively implementing those operational options which assure rapid success.[10] NATO can strengthen its conventional posture considerably by exploiting its technological superiority better than it traditionally has—in particular, by efficiently using modern technologies to perform key tasks.[11] The findings of the SDI research effort might contribute substantially to the rapid development and deployment of modern conventional systems.

Soviet Anti-Missile Capabilities. To undermine the effectiveness of NATO's strategy of "flexible response," the Soviet Union attaches particular importance to denying NATO the use of its nuclear options.

An essential element of NATO's strategic concept of flexible response is the "deliberate escalation" (e.g., raising the conflict to another level of intensity) in well-calculated, intentional steps—a strategy that operates independently from any threat of defeat at the conventional level. Selective use of nuclear weapons is geared to making the aggressor realize that no acceptable relation exists between his prospects of success and the risk he incurs—thus persuading him to discontinue his attack. NATO doctrine supports a quick cessation of hostilities where, if need be, the defender has the option of confronting the aggressor at a very early stage to restore deterrence. Options for the selective use of nuclear weapons, therefore, play a special part in NATO's nuclear plans.

According to expert estimates, the Soviet Union may have an anti-missile defense against the short- and intermediate-range systems stationed in Western Europe as early as the mid-1990s. The deployment of such a defense system could have grave consequences for the NATO strategy of "flexible response," depending on the efficiency of the Soviet defense system. Any restriction or even neutralization of NATO's options for selectively using its longer-range intermediate-range systems— Pershing II and cruise missiles—would cause the concept of "extended deterrence" to lose credibility.

The implications for the British and French nuclear potentials might be less aggravating, since their use would not normally fall into selective employment options (e.g., the use of a limited number of weapons with a limited range). In any case, the Soviet anti-missile defense system would have to achieve a very high level of efficiency to discredit British and French nuclear deterrence.

The development of effective Soviet anti-missile defense systems would also block potential NATO options for strengthening its conventional defense posture. NATO force modernization calls for using conventionally-armed ballistic missiles to neutralize the Warsaw Pact air forces and to delay, disrupt, and destroy follow-on forces. But the effectiveness of such systems would be seriously degraded by a Soviet "ATBM" capability.

The foregoing adverse implications for NATO's defense concept are, of course, not a consequence of the United States' Strategic Defense Initiative, as one hears time and again; rather they result from the buildup of Soviet anti-missile defenses—a long-standing effort which the Soviet Union will pursue, regardless of whether or not the United States continues its SDI research. If, however, the Soviet Union could unilaterally maintain a capability to ward off short- and intermediate-range missiles, the credibility of NATO's military strategic concept in Europe would fall into a regrettable plight.

Should the Soviet Union achieve a firm ATBM capability, NATO's spectrum of possible countermeasures would be limited. Attempts to overcome the enemy's defenses with more nuclear missiles, selectively employed, would run counter to any "selective use" doctrine.[12] Employing combat aircraft and cruise missiles for NATO's selective nuclear use is not a credible alternative, given the overall effectiveness of the Warsaw Pact air defense system. Unquestionably, strengthening NATO's conventional posture is an increasingly urgent responsibility, as well as countering the Soviet short- and intermediate-range systems.

Warsaw Pact Attack After Minimum Preparations. If the Soviet Union ever resorts to military aggression against NATO, the Soviet strategy would seek to defeat NATO in a swift conventional campaign, making maximum use of surprise at both the strategic and tactical level.[13] Quantitative and qualitative improvements in the Warsaw Pact's military potential have resulted in a growing Warsaw Pact capability to launch an attack after minimum preparations, thus allowing NATO the shortest possible warning. The Warsaw Pact's expanding offensive air power permits massive blows to NATO's air defenses, including those at interceptor-fighter air bases, at the very outset of hostilities. In contrast, the structural reforms of the Warsaw Pact ground forces have considerably improved their capability to conduct combined arms operations. The Warsaw Pact's continual fielding of new weapon systems—at shorter intervals than in NATO—has resulted in their greater combat effectiveness for rapid and deep thrusts into rear areas. Advances in command and control, fire direction, reconnaissance, and target acquisition enable the Warsaw Pact to conduct operations with greater flexibility than in the past.

The Warsaw Pact's peacetime deployment and state of readiness make NATO forces highly vulnerable to the Warsaw Pact's capability to launch an attack without prior reinforcement. Thus, NATO must upgrade conventional capabilities and minimize the probability of surprise. No improved conventional capabilities will pay adequate dividends if our forces are caught by surprise in their peacetime garrisons or during their deployment to defense areas.

Improvements in all-weather (day-and-night) surveillance, and especially our target-acquisition capabilities are of the greatest urgency, just as are the close links between national and NATO intelligence systems, and the coordinated evaluation of intelligence and the real-time data transmission. Minimizing the impact of a surprise attack calls for a high readiness of at least some portion of our defense forces; it requires rapid political decisions as well as the quasi-automatic release of specific, preplanned countermeasures. The latter include barrier and denial measures, dispersal of land and air forces, and direct defense. Furthermore, our forces must, better than in the past, be able to engage the enemy successfully even in surprise situations—using improved target acquisition.

A New Soviet Short- and Intermediate-Range Ballistic Missile Potential

The Soviet Union is currently adding a new dimension to its capability of launching an immediate attack. The Soviets are modernizing and expanding their shorter-range ballistic missile potential of FROG, SCUD, and SCALEBOARD systems which are organic to the Warsaw Pact divisions, as well as to the Soviet fronts. Their successor systems, the SS-21, SS-23 and SS-12/22, have a longer range and will one day have considerably improved accuracy. Furthermore, in contrast to the SCALEBOARD which has been fielded only in the Soviet Union, its successor system SS-12/22—with an extended range of 900 km—has also been deployed in the GDR and CSSR. Such forward stationing not only extends the effective range of these weapons systems, but deprives NATO of important early warning, since the Soviets no longer have to move these weapons forward prior to an attack.[14]

Excluding the SS-20, the Warsaw Pact has 1,685 shorter-range ballistic missiles at their disposal.[15] The number and range of these systems are more than sufficient to cover all primary targets in the Federal Republic of Germany and adjacent areas. In addition, the growing Warsaw Pact possesses improved cruise missiles and air-launched stand-off weapons which threaten essential targets in the rear of the European theater.

This new Warsaw Pact capability increases the nuclear threat to Europe to be sure; however, the decisive aspect of this threat is the improved accuracy expected from the ballistic, cruise, and stand-off-missile systems—specifically their effective use in a conventional configuration. This qualitative step forward by the Warsaw Pact could have disastrous consequences if it is not countered. As stated by the German Defense Minister Dr. Manfred Wörner:

> By concentrating missile strikes on prime NATO targets over massively attacking Warsaw Pact air and ground formations, the Soviet Union could prevent, delay or obstruct numerous NATO-response options in the critical initial phase of a conflict. Thus, an orderly mounting of NATO defensive operations with emphasis on forward defense, the inflow of ground and air reinforcements from abroad, freedom of maneuver in the rear areas, as well as the Alliance's capacity for nuclear response—above all the air-delivered components of that response—could be substantially disrupted and compromised, if not prevented entirely.[16]

The full extent of the new Warsaw Pact attack options with conventional missiles becomes obvious when paired with the increasing defensive capabilities of the Soviet Union, particularly against short- and mid-range missiles.

Again, this new dimension in the threat to Europe is not a consequence of SDI; it results from longstanding Soviet efforts to build up their offensive and defensive capabilities with the ever more conspicuous aim of denying effective response options to NATO.

The need to upgrade NATO's integrated air defense system in Europe to neutralize these new Warsaw Pact offensive options requires utmost urgency and must take place irrespective of whether or when the Strategic Defense Initiative becomes operational. Consequently, NATO has taken timely steps to evaluate the technological possibilities for upgrading of air defenses.[17]

The upgraded European air defense system must ward off ballistic, cruise, and stand-off missiles. For economic and military reasons, this program requires step-by-step improvements in existing air defense capabilities—chiefly incorporating the new anti-missile defenses into NATO's integrated air defense system. The anti-missile defense for Europe is a common task for the Alliance and not a "Euro-specific" program. The extended air defense system demands close cooperation with the United States. In fact, results of the current research for the strategic defense of the United States have great relevance for the buildup of an improved European air defense.

Harnessing SDI-Research Results to Strengthen Conventional Defense

Strengthening conventional defense continues to be a top priority in Europe, particularly in the eyes of the Federal Republic of Germany. In view of limited budgets and research, many people fear that competing demands for stronger conventional forces will be at odds with SDI development. The Supreme Allied Commander Europe has repeatedly voiced such concerns and admonished that "our nations must not let ADI divert their attention—and resources—from the prime need to improve our conventional forces."[18]

Others suggest that the technological breakthrough needed to successfully implement SDI will contribute greatly to the strengthening of our conventional defense, and will do so much earlier than expected. If this suggestion turns out to be true, it will largely determine the future attitude of an educated public in Western Europe toward SDI.

Prior to actual SDI employment, progress in sensor technology and signal processing could provide conventional NATO forces with effective real-time target acquisition—thus assuring a quantum jump in the better exploitation of available firepower. The use of such sensors for terminally guided ammunition would considerably increase the firepower of the NATO forces and would—combined with progress in target acquisition—offset the hitherto considerable superiority of the Warsaw Pact's conventional firepower.

Progress in the broad field of "Search, Acquisition, Tracking, and Kill Assessment (SATKA)" could serve the European missile defense as well as the Strategic Defense Initiative. Hyper-velocity missiles which have reached a high state of research are not only important ingredients of SDI, but also of an improved European air defense. In fact, electromagnetic guns could revolutionize the anti-armor battle long before they are deployed into space in an SDI framework.

The foregoing are but a few examples of how SDI research could contribute to strengthening the conventional defense and to opening new options for NATO as it battles to offset shifts in the balance of forces.

Numerous proposals from Western European experts suggest that NATO countries should pool their resources to strengthen the conventional defense in Europe, look for Euro-specific solutions to meet Euro-specific threats, and examine the prospects and requirements for a "European Defense Initiative (EDI)." However, such proposals suffer in two respects:

First, they ignore the necessity of close cooperation between Western Europe and the United States. Europe and the US must combine scarce resources and avoid duplication of research and development. Only through mutual cooperation can the technological "spin-offs" of SDI be fully harnessed for rapid and lasting improvements in our conventional defense. The United States has a genuine self-interest in the buildup of stronger conventional capabilities in Europe because the United States provides the second-strongest contingent for the conventional defense in Europe.

Second, an exclusive "European Defense Initiative" could easily be interpreted as a program intended to contrast the US "Strategic Defense Initiative," thus indicating a lack of support for SDI, even a tendency to dissociate from SDI. The debate about SDI is already fraught with divisiveness, and the Soviets will be very willing to drive a wedge between the United States and their West European allies over the issue of SDI. Conformity of the political will, unity of purpose, and concerted action are the bedrock of deterrence in Europe. The close cooperation between Western Europe and the United States—in SDI research as well as in strengthening the conventional defense in Europe—would be a striking demonstration of NATO's solidarity.

Franz-Joseph Schulze, retired General in the Bundeswehr of the Federal Republic of Germany, served in many NATO assignments to include Commander in Chief of Allied Forces Central Europe from 1977 to 1979 and Deputy Chief of Staff, Allied Command Europe, from 1973 to 1976. General Schulze has published widely on military issues to include articles in Foreign Affairs and Europa-Archiv.

NOTES

1. "The Security of the Federal Republic of Germany," *White Paper 1983* (Bonn: The Federal Minister of Defense, 1983), p. 52.

2. Fred S. Hoffman, "Nukleare Bedrohung, Sowjetische Macht und SDI," in *Europa-Archiv 21* (Bonn: Verlag Internationale Politik, 1985), p. 643 ff.

3. Paul Nitze in an address to the World Affairs Council on February 20, 1985; in *Europa-Archiv 6* (Bonn: Verlag Internationale Politik, 1985), p. D 184.

4. See *Soviet Strategic Defense Programs* (Washington, D.C.: U.S. Government Printing Office, October 1985), pp. 7 ff.

5. See *Soviet Military Power: 1985* (Washington, D.C.: U.S. Government Printing Office, 1985), p. 48.

6. Caspar W. Weinberger, address to the foreign press in Washington, D.C., on December 19, 1984; in *Europa-Archiv 6* (Bonn: Verlag Internationale Politik, 1985), p. D 151.

7. "The Security of the Federal Republic of Germany," *White Paper 1983* (Bonn: The Federal Minister of Defense, 1983), para 66.

8. General Bernard W. Rogers, "The Atlantic Alliance: Prescriptions for a Difficult Decade," *Foreign Affairs* (Summer 1982), p. 1151.

9. Ibid.

10. See *European Security Study*, "Strengthening Conventional Deterrence in Europe" (ESECS) (London: Macmillan Press, 1983), p. 18.

11. *European Security Study*, "Strengthening Conventional Deterrence in Europe" (ESECS II) (Boulder and London: Westview Press, 1985), p. 1.

12. Konrad Seitze, "Die Zukunft von Sicherheit und Abrüstung in Europa" (The future of security and disarmament in Europe), *Europa-Archiv 3* (Bonn: Verlag Internationale Politik, 1986)

13. *European Security Study*, "Strengthening Conventional Deterrence in Europe" (ESECS II) (Boulder: Westview Press, 1985), p. 2.

14. "The Situation and the Development of the Federal Armed Forces," *White Paper 1985* (Bonn: The Federal Minister of Defense, 1985) p. 56.

15. *The Military Balance 1985* (London: The International Institute for Strategic Studies, 1985), p. 158 ff. The number includes the older systems as far as they are still in service and their successors.

16. Manfred Worner, "A Missile Defense for NATO-Europe," *Strategic Review* (Winter 1986), p. 55.

17. E.g., AAS-20 Study, "Antitactical Ballistic Missile System Concepts," initiated by the Advisory Group for Aerospace Research and Development (AGARD) in 1983.

18. General Bernard W. Rogers, "SDI and the Security of Europe," an address to the Liberal Society of Research and Lectures, The European Institute for Peace and Security, and The American-European Community Association, Brussels, 27 February 1986.

PART IV

WILL WE BE MORE SECURE
IN 2010?
THREE VIEWS

WILL WE BE MORE SECURE IN 2010?

Robert W. Komer

The effect of a successful SDI program will be quixotic. We will probably end up making non-nuclear war more feasible at a time when the enormous costs of doing so will seriously reduce US capabilities for deterring or fighting conventional wars. The United States will probably be in a materially more difficult security situation than today.

Background and Assumptions

The assumption is that, by 2010, we move to a "defensively-dominant strategic environment," which means that the American SDI works and is fully deployed.

This scenario does not mean that strategic defenses have completely replaced deterrence—only that the mix of means for achieving deterrence has changed. The difference is one of means, not ends.

My paper is based on three complementary assumptions. First, I assume SDI works for the Soviets too, and they have similarly deployed it. In the more than 40 years since World War II, the Soviets have quickly caught up with every Western weapon system, except big aircraft carriers, and they now are building these, too. Also, according to the Reagan Administration, the Soviets are working to develop anti-missile defenses at least as hard as we are. Moreover, the Reagan Administration has several times suggested that we might be willing to "share" defensive technology with the Soviet Union.

Second, I assume that a defensively dominated strategic environment is not confined to the United States and the USSR, but extends to their major allies. In short, at least NATO Europe and Japan have also deployed strategic defenses over 25 years, while the Soviets deploy defenses to cover their Warsaw Pact allies.

Third, the overall US costs of a full-scale "strategic shield" will be at least one trillion dollars, as two former secretaries of defense have suggested. In the meantime, Soviet costs will at least be comparable to ours.

Transition to a defensively dominant strategic environment would indeed add up to a major change in US defense concepts. We do not fully realize today that—even though the USSR probably reached rough strategic parity by the early 1970s—15 years later the threat of US strategic retaliation remains the chief component of extended deterrence. Offensive retaliation still works in protecting vital US interests, and will likely do so until SDI is presumably deployed.

On the other hand, except at sea, in no major overseas theater could the United States and its allies be called conventionally superior or even equal to the USSR. Our military capabilities are imbalanced compared to Moscow, especially on the conventional side. Only the nuclear deterrent makes the difference for Japan and NATO—and probably for the Persian Gulf as well.

The Soviet Union is in a very different position from NATO in this respect. Its more balanced buildup has always stressed conventional as well as nuclear forces. Except at sea (where the United States is dominant), the Soviets have clear conventional superiority in all the Eurasian rimlands. Thus, if SDI becomes reality, its strategic position would be less radically affected than that of the United States.

Cost is also an important factor. The Administration has made no estimate of total life cycle costs, aside from a 1984 estimate that $26 billion in R&D funds would be needed simply to prove feasibility between 1984-1990. However, former Secretary of Defense Harold Brown has estimated that $500 billion to a trillion dollars might be necessary to develop and deploy a full "umbrella-type" defense of the sort President Reagan initially proposed. Let's accept this estimate as a reasonable ballpark figure until better ones emerge.

Given current resource constraints, stimulated by high federal deficits, such defense costs will be hard to fund. Even though Moscow gives higher priority to defense spending than Washington, sums of this size for strategic defenses would also be difficult for the USSR to fund.

Another consideration is how many, if any, nuclear weapons are likely to be retained in 2010, after fully developed strategic defenses have been installed. True, we can assume continued East-West competition for the next 25 years, though it is hard to predict what crisis would lead to US-Soviet war—unless the very process of transition toward a defensively dominated strategic environment were responsible.

Of course, the strategic defenses of the United States (and the USSR) would protect them against other nuclear powers as well. But this situation hardly exhausts the number of situations in which French, Chinese, or Indian weaponry could exert great influence.

It is by no means clear that China, India, or France would give up their nuclear weapons just because the superpowers did so. Their possibilities for developing or funding credible shields are certainly far less than those of the superpowers. Thus, we will live in a much less stable strategic environment than at present. Given such a situation, the United States and the USSR will undoubtedly retain a certain minimum strategic nuclear capability.

Presumably both superpowers will also retain "battlefield" nuclear capabilities. Shooting down ballistic missiles or bombers is far different than shooting down artillery shells or rockets or even short-range missiles where the time factor is far shorter. Thus, this paper assumes that both superpowers will retain the "battlefield" nuclear systems, perhaps up to an agreed range.

Thus, even if a defensively dominant strategic environment occurs in 2010, both superpowers might opt to retain certain nuclear capabilities—though not necessarily as large or varied as now. The USSR has traditionally been reluctant to dispose of old weaponry, and the United States might choose to retain a comparable stockpile precisely because the Soviets were doing so. Agreed US/USSR arms controls might modify this projection somewhat, but we can not make accurate predictions. The coming of SDI might induce more movement toward arms controls and increase US insistence on verification measures, since the squirrelling away of a few weapons by cheating would be so dangerous.

Likely Security Situation in 2010

Having defined these additional assumptions, we can now address its likely dimensions.

1. What Would Strategic Defenses Buy Us? Undoubtedly, the existence of credible strategic defenses by the year 2010 would be extremely valuable to the United States even if the USSR had a similar system. Ever since World War II, US security strategy has been aimed primarily at deterrence, backed up primarily by massive nuclear capabilities. Soviet SDI would remove this main force of US deterrent strategy. In return, the United States would have more security against Soviet nuclear attack—the one threat which has worried us most since Soviet acquisition of comparable strategic nuclear capabilities. Presumably, these defenses would be against air as well as missile attack. Whatever the cost, they would relieve us of the threat we most fear—the critical threat to the US homeland.

In one way, SDI would strengthen our extended deterrent umbrella over our allies. They would be far less likely to fear that the United States would not respond militarily to an attack on them because of its fear of nuclear devastation to itself. But how meaningful would our umbrella be if the USSR also had an anti-nuclear shield? We currently have pretty reliable, if not wholly credible, deterrence because of our capability to retaliate. So, too, does the Soviet Union. Despite the Soviets having overtaken us in nuclear capabilities, the current reasonably stable nuclear balance seems likely to remain strong. Indeed, the only serious possibility of "breakout" on either side seems to lie in SDI itself. And, by 2010, even if the United States had "broken out" with effective strategic defenses, the USSR would probably catch up within three to five years.

2. *What About Deterring Non-Nuclear War?* Unfortunately, a defensively dominant strategic nuclear environment might undermine deterrence of conventional war. Indeed, the very nature of extended deterrence probably would change. We must remember that every single conflict in the first 40 years of the nuclear age has been conventional.

This shift would be very important for the United States, because our vital interests are not confined to defending the US homeland against nuclear attack. Soviet achievement of dominance over such vital areas as Western Europe, Japan, or the oil-rich Persian Gulf would radically change the global balance of power. Thus, deterring Soviet attack in these areas has been a vital US interest. In fact, we went to war in 1917 and 1941 to prevent precisely such a shift in the overall balance of power. Since then we have wisely extended our commitment to NATO and Japan, and backed it up with large overseas deployments. Extended deterrence has worked, based primarily on our nuclear capabilities.

But by 2010 the emergence of strategic defenses would tend to undermine this means of deterrence. In effect, *the world will be made safer for conventional war.* The situation will resemble 1945-1985, when the only wars fought were relatively minor, non-nuclear ones. What would change would be our ability to deter such conflicts—and possible direct confrontation between the superpowers.

The risk arises chiefly from the non-nuclear superiority of Soviet conventional forces around the Eurasian rimlands, from China-Japan to Europe. Will this situation endure until 2010? The only safe bet is to assume it will, because, in all likelihood, the USSR will keep outspending America, Europe, and Japan on conventional forces. The United States, NATO, and Japan have never sought to compete in this arena (except at sea), preferring to rely (successfully) on nuclear deterrence. Would the USSR remain reluctant to use conventional military pressure if credible deterrence no longer existed? No one can say, but we can assume that Moscow would be more willing to seize opportunities than at present.

A revolution in conventional military technology is underway, second only to the actual nuclear and missile revolution. Technology is changing the face of the modern battlefield. Here again, however, the USSR is generally keeping pace with the West, despite the latter's technological lead. Moreover, technology impact must be measured, not in terms of laboratory demonstrations, but in terms of usable weapons deployed.

Could arms controls limit this new dimension of threat? Of course they could, and in 25 years much is possible. Bilateral arms control agreements could lead to substantial cuts in US/USSR strategic nuclear weapons. The value of such weapons would decline as strategic defenses were erected. We must realize, however, that we do not live in a wholly bipolar nuclear world. Four other countries now have modest nuclear weapon capabilities, and others are capable of developing them. Would a decline in the crushing superiority of the two superpowers lead to further proliferation? Moreover, it is hard to envisage the Soviet Union agreeing to any serious limits in the non-nuclear field where it is superior, unless the United States made comparable concessions. The only real non-nuclear arms control negotiation has been going on now for 13 long years.

3. *The Impact of High SDI Costs.* The United States, Japan, and NATO can compete effectively with the USSR

in the non-nuclear arms arena. The trouble is the will is lacking, a factor that is highly unlikely to change in the next 25 years. Historically speaking, democratic societies have traditionally been reluctant to spend enough on defense in peacetime, frequently resulting in their having to pay far higher costs when unpreparedness leads to war. Such has been the case in all four large American 20th-century conflicts. Europe's defense effort has been even less satisfactory than America's, and Japan's modest effort since World War II is almost a caricature.

Today another cost factor depressing defense spending is the deficit spending problem. Japan, the United States, France, and other NATO allies are confronting high government deficits and avoiding excessive public spending. It will take years to reduce these deficits to tolerable levels. The US Congress has even mandated automatic cuts via the Gramm-Rudman process, if it does not cut each annual budget enough. Gramm-Rudman—which would affect SDI if its formula for across-the-board funding cuts ever becomes operative—will almost certainly prevent increased defense spending until the deficit is substantially reduced. At the same time, the President and the Secretary of Defense will continue giving SDI first priority for defense outlays. Under these circumstances the only logical way to fund SDI, at least in the near future, will be largely through tradeoffs. In short, SDI will be funded largely at the expense of other defense needs.

Moreover, conventional spending has always been far higher than nuclear spending in every nuclear power's defense budget. In every case, however, nuclear spending has received first priority. Now SDI is sharing this top priority in the United States, and may do so in other countries too. Under these circumstances, a half a trillion or trillion dollar US investment in strategic defense almost certainly will not be funded as an add-on but will compete with conventional (and for a period, nuclear) forces for available funds. The former will certainly win during the years of the Reagan Administration, and probably afterward too, unless SDI clearly becomes impractical as a technology. If not, after a while SDI will have achieved such momentum that it will be extremely hard to turn off.

The likely result in 2010 will be that, just when strategic defenses are making the world safe for conventional war, their staggering cost will cripple Western ability to compete effectively in conventional forces. It is impracticable to determine which non-nuclear capabilities will be hit hardest 25 years from now.

Of course, the USSR will not be wholly free of economic or social pressure for lower defense outlays. Many argue that declining Soviet GNP and productivity growth will prohibit Moscow from continuing to give top priority to its burgeoning defense effort. Gorbachev will not likely risk the politically dangerous reforms essential to further Soviet growth, and it is possible that over the next 25 years the Soviet Union will have to cut back somewhat on defense spending. In its crudest form, one can argue that the West could spend the Soviet Union into bankruptcy, or at least force it to change its resource allocations. The appeal of this argument, however, flies in the face of experience. Given the way the USSR *has* managed to control consumption and to fund massive military investment for decades, we can only assume that it will continue to do so. However, a trillion rubles or so for strategic defenses would probably be funded in part by trade-offs rather than further milking of the civilian economy (but doubtless less so than Western SDI programs).

4. The Diffusion of Power. A slow diffusion of power has been occurring on the world scene. Increasingly, the United States finds itself competing with other major powers since the end of World War II. The postwar decolonization process has created dozens of new countries, though mostly of modest potential. Comparatively speaking, the Japanese have become the free world's second-ranked economic power, and the United States has had to share power not only with the USSR, but nations like Japan, China, India, Brazil, and the Europeans. Only in the nuclear arena does clear differentiation separate the superpowers from the rest of the world.

Now this distinction too would be partly effaced if a defensively dominant strategic environment comes to pass. The United States and the USSR would be less able to deter other powers by brandishing their superior nuclear capabilities. Thus, more wars and more crises between non-superpowers are likely to take place.

If this situation occurs, it will likely exert an adverse impact on the cohesion of our alliances. Inter-allied differences have already occurred, particularly over US use of its power in the Third World (as in the recent Libyan case). In every case, however, our allies have bowed to the US-extended deterrent umbrella. If that umbrella is no longer available, our allies will be more inclined to press their differences, and may even withdraw from alliances. Moreover, a Soviet-type SDI shield will make the British and French nuclear deterrent shields almost useless, a prospect which has already made them unhappy.

5. *Theater Deterrence*. Experience suggests it would be much harder for NATO as a whole to fund a European NATO strategic defense than for the US to fund one for its own homeland. Moreover, the deployment process would take longer. If we assume that NATO and Japan have fully developed strategic defenses, these defenses would presumably protect them from nuclear attack. If they do not, then they would be much more vulnerable. So too would be most other US friends or allies.

We must also consider that strategic defenses would not directly protect against battlefield nuclear weapons. Indeed, such defenses might actually lead to increased use of battlefield nuclear weapons, particularly in border areas between NATO and the Warsaw Pact. Further, there could well be a shift in funding from strategic nuclear to tactical nuclear. In some respects such a development would tend to reduce the impact of some of the other effects mentioned above. It might also enhance nuclear proliferation.

6. *Impact on Stability.* At least to date, the nuclear world has been a surprisingly stable one. No direct superpower armed clash has occurred. Nor does one seem likely. However, if the present diffusion of power continues and if a dominant defensive environment emerges, reduced superpower nuclear superiority could lead to a more volatile, fractious, and unstable world. A civilization-crushing massive nuclear exchange would no longer be likely, but small non-nuclear wars—perhaps large ones—are more likely to occur. How well is the United States equipped to face a more volatile security environment, with many more calls on its resources?

Conclusion

We must be cautious about drawing large generalizations about what will occur 25 years from now and about predicting the impact of technologies whose impact we see only dimly. History suggests that nations have frequently missed many of the longer-term implications of major technological change.

Still, I have argued that the advent of a defensively dominant strategic environment will probably have several adverse implications whose magnitudes are difficult to predict. In a very real sense, SDI would tend to make the world "safe" for conventional war—an arena in which the USSR has several major advantages.

Unquestionably, the Soviets have superiority in most non-nuclear capabilities, except at sea. Such capabilities are made more serious by the geopolitical location of the USSR in the heartland of the crucial Eurasian continent, around which (in the Eurasian rimlands) lie most of the overseas areas of vital interest to the United States. These areas (Western Europe, Northeast Asia, and the Persian Gulf oil region) are adjacent to

Soviet land/air power, but far from the remote United States.

Extended US nuclear deterrence has provided a security umbrella around the world. Any development which seriously reduces such effectiveness makes Eurasia more vulnerable to the USSR, and less susceptible to US support. Nor can US naval superiority make much difference, as it could in meeting threats to areas remote from Eurasia—such as Africa, Australia, or the Western Hemisphere.

Of course, the United States and its allies could meet this threat by extensively building up their conventional defenses. However, neither Japan nor Western Europe, indeed not even the United States, has shown much willingness to try to cope with the conventional Soviet threat. Nor are they likely to do so in the future.

The huge cost of strategic defenses will accentuate this problem. Most Western defense spending today is conventional rather than nuclear. Moreover, given the pressures to reduce state deficits, much, if not most, of the trillion dollar cost to fully develop strategic systems will be funded by trade-offs from other defense programs instead of new money. Thus, making the United States and its allies safe from nuclear devastation will come at the cost of increasing the likelihood of conventional war. SDI-type programs will also make the US and its allies less capable of coping with conventional conflicts. In short, the costs of SDI itself may make it exceedingly difficult to deter conventional war.

By the same token, removing the US extended deterrent umbrella will make its allies more vulnerable—ironically, at a time when the United States will be even more dependent on these allies for conventional coalition defense.

The current, comparatively stable strategic world of nuclear standoff would become less stable and more volatile if conventional war risks and costs again became dominant. The USSR might become more aggressive, as might numerous other states. Although arms controls might become more feasible, especially in the nuclear field, they will be insufficient to cause real change.

In sum, the one overriding advantage of anti-nuclear defenses—that they remove the threat of nuclear devastation of the developed world—would bring with it some very tricky side effects. In short, the "cure" of SDI might be worse than controlling the "disease" of current strategic nuclear parity.

Robert W. Komer is currently a consultant with the RAND Corporation. He has held numerous influential positions in the US government. From 1979-81 he was Undersecretary of Defense for Policy. Before that he held positions at the Central Intelligence Agency and National Security Council Staff; and has served as Deputy Special Assistant and then Special Assistant to the President for National Security Affairs, Deputy to the Commander, US Military Assistance Command, Vietnam, and Ambassador to Turkey. He holds an S.B. and M.B.A. from Harvard University and has written extensively on strategy and defense affairs, including his recent book Maritime Strategy or Coalition Defense.

WILL WE BE MORE SECURE IN 2010?

Albert Gore, Jr.

"Will we be more secure in the year 2010?" To attempt to answer such a question seems at first glance to be an exercise in *hubris*. Twenty years is an exceptionally long time about which to make any serious estimate, particularly when the more modest 10-year horizon of many national intelligence estimates has frequently turned out to be overly ambitious.

On the other hand, it now takes about a decade to deploy a new strategic weapons system, which then may have an operational lifetime of 15 years or more. As for arms control, even controversial agreements such as the SALT Interim Agreement and the ABM Treaty are proving to be very durable: about 15 years have passed since they were signed under conditions depicted as provisional—yet both treaties are still with us.

In other words, upon reflection, one finds it isn't so unreasonable to ask for a look 20 years into the future. We have all the more reason to do so today when we consider that we are now making decisions on the long-range shape of our strategic forces. Current modernization plans involving the Advanced Technology Bomber (ATB) and Trident, for example, will not be fully operational until the late 1990s. US decisions on a mobile missile are still pending, but a go-ahead could well result in substantial numbers of missiles coming into service toward the end of the century.

Of tremendous import, of course, is the Strategic Defense Initiative. SDI's research phase alone might bring us close to the year 2000, perhaps synchronizing with several waves of deployments at increasing levels of technological sophistication. That process might not be completed even by the year 2010 although, in a manner of speaking, SDI is already a source of leverage on the future.

Thus, if the 20-year scope of this discussion is reasonable, what about the terms of reference? How, for example, can we give clarity and meaning to a word like "safe?"

Let's begin with what Gene Rostow called the "geopolitical radiation" of nuclear weapons. This very handy term encompasses all those aspects of nuclear weapons not found in weapons-effects charts: the access they provide to Great Power status; the risk that imbalances of relatively little military importance might inspire risk-taking rather than risk-averting behavior—thereby increasing the risk of war.

Relatively inconsequential military changes in the US-Soviet strategic balance could produce political changes that might make the world less safe for us. Until recently, we took it for granted that we would always find the political will and the financial means to forestall this kind of risk. That assumption needs to be reexamined. The Reagan deficit looms over all defense spending, including funds for strategic weapons, in a way which could—for the first time—leave the United States Government unable to keep up with the Soviets should they decide to break out of existing constraints.

Still, suppose we somehow avoid these perils. Let's assume we are free to consider the essence of safety in the nuclear age and to examine various circumstances in which we might find ourselves by the year 2010.

In my opinion, what passes for "safety" is summed up by the term "stability." I use the word "stability" to describe a situation in which two conditions are satisfied: first, *neither* side, looking at its own forces, will find the means to carry out a first strike to its own advantage; and second, *neither* side, looking at the *other's* forces, will find there a workable first-strike capability.

Please note that I use the concept of stability in a manner which implies that it is a mutual—not a unilateral—context. Many people still think a stable world is one in which we can amass the means to threaten the

Soviets, but not vice versa. Even some opponents of the MX, for example, would be content to deploy at sea a much larger force of D-5 missiles than now planned, which would be vulnerable to Soviet attack—though able to threaten most of the Soviet Union's hardened strategic targets. It seems to me, however, that stability is either mutual or nonexistent. Either *both* countries find themselves relatively at ease on the question of the first-strike capabilities of the other, or *both* countries are involved in an unstable nuclear relationship.

Two Paths to Mutual Stability

Basically, there are two ways to arrive at a condition of mutual stability: defense dominance or offense dominance—Star Wars or Deterrence.

Defense Dominance. Let us begin by looking first at the notion of defense-dominance, since it is the theoretical underpinning of President Reagan's dream of a world where nuclear weapons are impotent and obsolete.

Copious literature is available on the subject of Star Wars' technological riskiness, and I don't intend to add to it here. Much less is known about the financial implications of a full Star Wars defense, but that picture is beginning to change. And none too soon, since the price tag for a highly effective defense—assuming that technology is not a problem—could easily come to the fantastic sum of a trillion dollars.

Again, however, let us assume that we can overcome these difficulties. Let's search for a more abstract truth. If tomorrow we could exchange today's offense-dominant world for one which is defense-dominant, then we would achieve stability levels unattainable merely by reshaping our offensive forces. However, we cannot simply pass through the gates to an immediate state of nuclear grace; instead, we must traverse a narrow and hazardous path.

Obviously, the process of deploying a strategic defense requires many years of effort. During that time, one must assume that both sides are willing to tolerate a transition period where their existing strategic forces become progressively less effective. Unfortunately, from each side's perspective, the effectiveness of its own forces will appear to decline while those of the opponent will appear to grow.

No less an authority than the President appears to have grasped that the combination of partial defenses and strong offenses is potentially explosive: intensely destabilizing because such a situation encourages an effective first-strike capability. Long before we attain the level of "mutual assured survival" through defenses, we would reach a state of what is called a "splendid first-strike capability"—the means to attack the enemy's nuclear forces, and then use defenses to sop up his disorganized (or "ragged") response.

This realization led the President to the rather shocking conclusion that defenses ought not to go up until we and the Soviets had completely eliminated all nuclear arsenals, a formulation so radical that it had to be quickly explained away by others whose job is to tidy up these things. The President, however, was not wrong; he was merely describing with less than perfect elegance how the nuclear forces of both sides would interact during a prolonged transition towards a defense-dominant condition.

In so doing, he was also explaining why it strains credulity to assume that SDI can be pursued for long without setting off competitive efforts to build up offensive forces *and* to create increasingly effective means for neutralizing defensive systems.

The President was also, in effect, explaining why the various lesser forms of SDI—now increasingly under consideration—are not desirable. The stripped-down early technology version, which General Abrahamson is promoting for the 1990s, will inescapably lead to a highly destabilizing force with first-strike potential.

Were positions reversed, we would not for a moment tolerate having the Soviet Union lecture us about the benefits of a space-based defense. It astounds me to hear senior officials of this Administration testify before Congress that the Soviets need not be alarmed by what we are doing because they "know" that the US would never contemplate a first strike. In the nuclear age, capabilities speak louder than statements of intent.

Offensive Dominance. The other route to stability involves combining modernization and arms control, within the context of a nuclear balance which remains offense-dominant.

We can have nuclear offensive forces which are sufficiently diverse and resistant to first strike so that each side feels confident in its ability to retaliate, but not in its ability to mount a successful first strike. Such a situation may exist even with relatively high numbers of weapons, although the long argument over the "window of vulnerability" shows that numbers alone are not enough. Stability can also exist with much lower levels of forces but, of course, at progressively lower levels stability is harder to achieve even in purely theoretical terms.

In either case, a common denominator is a need for mobility. Mobile ICBMs are the key to stable nuclear relationships, where neither side ever has even a theoretically convincing first-strike capability. To destroy mobile missiles requires not a point attack, but a barrage. Under conditions of a barrage, the *defender* can drive the requirement in warheads or throw-weight to a level beyond the attacker's means.

Mobile ICBMs relieve arms controllers of the intolerable burden they have had to carry until now—the burden of providing survivable land-based forces. Instead, mobility, coupled with force modernization, will enforce stability. Moreover, the threshold for achieving stability no longer begins after completing deep reductions; it exists at today's level of forces as measured by the total ballistic missile throw-weight of

each side, providing mobiles are introduced. Furthermore, such a mobile missile concept reveals the Far
Right's incessant attack on SALT II to be absurd.

If the President does away with SALT, or even
"merely" suspends its operation until the Soviets satisfy
our concerns regarding compliance, we shall, for the
first time in 15 years, have no arrangement in place to
constrain the US-Soviet nuclear rivalry. Advocates of this
course contend we don't need to fear what the Soviets
will do. We are told that Soviet requirements for nuclear
weapons are satisfactory at existing levels and, in any
event, that their plans for weapons are already bounded
by the next Soviet Five-Year Plan, if not by arms control.

Regardless of what one thinks about this argument's
merit, it represents a gamble of incredible proportions.
If the Soviets decide to increase their forces, they have
the means to do so massively and rapidly. We, I am
sure, could keep pace—but the best we could hope for
would be to maintain parity at some multiple of today's
inventory of nuclear weapons.

These annual crises we are having about SALT
involve a decision of very large proportions—one which
affected not only arms control prospects in the final
months of the former Administration, but also will affect
it long afterward—possibly to the year 2010. Moreover,
we must understand that President Reagan was being
urged to act on other issues of comparable significance
to arms control and nuclear policy.

Regarding the ABM Treaty, for example, clearly certain Administration officials will never be satisfied until
it has either been abrogated or neutered. In 1986, the
Administration took a major step in this direction by
embracing a new legal interpretation of the Treaty,
essentially tossing it aside as a constraint upon SDI. The
Administration tempered this interpretation by an-
nouncing it would nonetheless continue to pursue SDI
as though the ABM Treaty's legal meaning had remained
unchanged. This policy has already come under attack
on the grounds that it will interfere with the efficiency
of SDI research.

Were the President to act on this advice, he would again be inviting the Soviets to take reprisals: to multiply the number of their weapons to offset our anticipated defenses; to improve and expand their anti-satellite capability to attack our defenses; and to deploy more conventional defenses against ballistic missiles on a crash basis. We, meanwhile, are a decade away from knowing whether Star Wars is scientifically possible—let alone feasible—to deploy.

As for nuclear modernization, the President is likewise being urged to embark upon a radical change of course. Earlier in this decade, the country was in the throes of a major political upheaval about force modernization, a debate which came to a white hot focus on the MX. At its height, the battle for the MX challenged President Reagan's overall conduct of US-Soviet affairs: his defeat, which was imminent on several occasions, would have damaged not just his nuclear policy but his presidency.

In the end, Congress decided to limit the MX modernization to 50 and to proceed with developing the Midgetman missile. That MX missile compromise represented the most that its advocates could secure and the furthest its enemies could suppress it. The idea of the single-warhead Midgetman, meanwhile, was the one concept which all participants in the debate were able to agree: an island of consensus in an ocean of dispute.

However, President Reagan was told that this outcome can be reversed: that Congress was ready to approve another 50 MX missiles and to indefinitely delay final decisions on the Midgetman, beyond the next national election. This position, too, comes from those who have worked assiduously to get rid of SALT constraints and to undermine the ABM Treaty.

If the President heeds this advice, he risks tearing apart the one aspect of weapons' policy and arms control where he enjoys reasonable support. The most likely outcome would be to disrupt plans for ICBM modernization of *any* sort, and to rekindle sharp debate about all other nuclear programs as well. Continued debate hinders our national interest, particularly since Soviet modernization programs will continue to advance while we argue among ourselves.

There is a temptation to see all of this as the kind of folly whose origins David Stockman would well understand. But I believe the truth is even more disquieting. Serious as they are, these disputes over arms control and nuclear policy have roots that go even deeper, down to the most profound schisms in American thinking about how to deal with the Soviet Union.

The Soviet Union, SALT, and US Security

At issue is whether we can best safeguard the security of the United States by trying to stabilize its strategic relations with the Soviet Union under mutually-agreeable terms, or whether we can only be secure if we "outlive" the Soviet Union as it exists today.

The Reagan Administration characteristically discounted the value of any *modus vivendi* with the Soviets because it did not believe a satisfactory arrangement was possible—or, even if achieved, that it would not be honored for very long. Ideologues of the Far Right see a world where our struggle with communism can end favorably only if the Soviets undergo a radical transformation. American strategy, as they prescribe it, must relentlessly seek to induce that crisis by forcing the Soviet system to operate under more stress than it can reasonably tolerate.

From the Far Right perspective, arms control is debilitating, with minor successes only lulling us to forget that a larger struggle for survival is underway. The last thing the Far Right wants is to codify a better US-Soviet nuclear relationship through arms control. Instead, it wants to overturn the present balance in favor of a restored American dominance, which they consider both feasible and necessary.

The proposals before the ending Reagan Administration represented the agenda of those who reject the pursuit of stability in favor of the dream of dominance. The Far Right wanted us to challenge the Soviets in a high-stakes game, assuming the Soviets lack the endurance to keep up with us and in the hope that they might damage themselves in the process.

It is too much to ask that the President have the expertise to deal with such theories. But it may not be too much to hope that he has the wisdom to see the sheer and desperate risk of it all. The President must continue to comply with SALT II and the stabilities it provides: the US may dismantle two Poseidon submarines to compensate for the new Trident boat.

Heated rhetoric continues to be exchanged on the subject of arms control, mobile missiles, modernization, and SDI. I would like to add to our store of facts and insight on this issue—using some excellent computer studies done for me by the Congressional Research Service.

These studies examine three long-range possibilities. First, we might stop dismantling launchers exclusively for SALT reasons. Second, we would dismantle launchers and do it by taking out Poseidons—which is the precedent already established by the Reagan Administration. Third, we would comply by dismantling—except that we would make sure we picked a dismantling strategy that worked best for us.

Let me add that, in all three cases, we would be carrying out a most vigorous modernization program involving:

- deploying 50 MX missiles;
- deploying 500 Midgetman missiles;
- converting 194 B-52s to ALCM carriers;
- deploying 100 B-1 bombers;

- subsequently converting those B-1s to ALCM carriers;
- deploying 132 Stealth bombers; and
- deploying a total of 20 Trident submarines carrying a total of 480 Trident II missiles.

(We are also planning to deploy hundreds of land-attack sea-launch cruise missiles that are nuclear-armed, but these are not under discussion because they are not accountable under SALT.)

If we stop dismantling forces, then our arsenal of warheads increases for a time. Eventually, though, we will have to retire forces because of their age. Eventually, these retirements will force our totals down, even though modernization will put substantial numbers of new forces into our inventory. Between now and 2000, our warhead totals would peak in 1992 and then decline to a level just a bit higher than the mid-1980s. Meanwhile, for this gain, we must accept the risk of an all-out competition with the Soviets.

In other words, it doesn't pay to junk the SALT limits.

An Optimal US Strategy

Thus, we should well question whether there is an optimal strategy for dismantling—if we are going to stay with SALT for the long term. I believe there is such a strategy, and one based on taking our SALT reductions in such a way that we retain the most survivable warheads for the longest period of time.

The mechanics of it are clear enough, based on my speech for the Congressional Record three years ago and my colleague, Senator Nunn, who incorporated his views in his letter to the President on SALT compliance.

Specifically, we should not dismantle Poseidons early on. Instead, we should take our cuts for as long as we can from a mix of older systems such as Titan and

Polaris (or from less-survivable, less-highly MIRV'd weapons such as the Minuteman III (specifically, from those Minuteman IIIs that have the Mark 12, rather than the superior Mark 12a warhead).

If we defer the dismantling of Poseidons as long as possible, we can retain approximately 1000 SLBM warheads in service for almost a decade. In other words, we can substantially increase survivable SLBM warheads in our forces during this period—to a point where very highly survivable, follow-on systems (such as Midgetman, Stealth, and more Trident submarines) become available.

SALT II has been the *de facto* policy of the United States since 1979, and yet its continuity is doubtful because the President did not recognize its merits: it is the one bridge we have to a safer future. Destroy SALT and the ABM Treaty and we shall know a world in 2010 which will be far more dangerous than today. Retain them, and they become the foundation for what the President once said he wanted: stability, accompanied by deep cuts in offensive forces.

We can gain that stability if both sides agree to introduce mobile ICBMs under controlled conditions that keep the SALT framework intact. As for deep reductions, the Soviet Union's asking price involves the complete dismantling of SDI—a strategy where the Soviets clearly overreach themselves. Suppose, however, they can be bargained down to mutual and verifiable constraints on research which permit vigorous programs to continue—but reinforce the barriers against development and deployment? If so, the resulting agreement would close the circle and lead us, by 2010, to a world that would indeed have a safer stability.

What, finally, is the Soviet Union's role in all this? The United States owes the world an approach to safety in the nuclear age that shows restraint and wisdom. Most emphatically, we do not owe the Soviet Union any kind of therapy at our expense for their national obsession with security and secrecy. If they continue to come forward with clumsily camouflaged traps for us and our allies, we must reject what they offer. If they play loose with us about compliance, we should hammer at that theme and protect our interests.

But we ourselves have shifted too often: we have not followed through on signed agreements; we've switched our signals and linked and de-linked negotiations on strategic forces to extraneous issues. The hopes we have for a safer world in 2010 rest on our greater maturity and the accompanying arms control agreements we negotiate with the Soviets.

Albert Gore, Jr., United States Senator from Tennessee since 1984, served in the US House of Representatives from 1976 to 1982. Senator Gore holds a BA degree from Harvard University and has attended the Graduate School of Religion and the Law School at Vanderbilt University. Since his appointment to the House Intelligence Committee in 1980, Mr. Gore has devoted a great deal of attention to arms control matters, outlining his proposals in the New Republic *(May 5, 1982).*

WILL WE BE MORE SECURE IN 2010?

Eugene V. Rostow

I can easily answer the question whether we shall be more secure in 2010: personally, I shall certainly be more secure by 2010. But the planners of this book probably had something else in mind. I suspect they mean by their question, "Will the United States be more secure because of the SDI program?"

My answer is, "Yes, somewhat, assuming that the rest of our security policy is reasonably sensible."[1]

Some Assumptions

In facing the future, we must make some assumptions or conjectures. The first is that SDI will succeed, and that it will lead to our developing one or more weapon systems that meet Paul Nitze's tests of economy and efficiency. The next assumption is that, while these systems will not provide complete coverage of the United States, Europe, Japan and other areas, they will provide at least enough protection to destroy a considerable fraction—say, 50 percent—of potential attacking missiles, whether the new systems operate at the boost phase, mid-flight, or as protection for our deployed weapons—or indeed at all three levels.

Second, we must make some reasonable political assumptions. Undoubtedly, some changes in the structure and dynamics of world politics will occur during the next 22 years; we do not yet know what they are. Therefore let us assume that there will be no revolution in the Soviet Union and no breakup of the Soviet state into a dozen or more national states, but that by 2010, we shall confront the same Soviet Union we have known since 1917—expansionist, highly militarized, unreconstructed.

Let us assume also that our relations with Canada, Europe, Japan, and China are still what they are today.

That is a realistic hypothesis, once we assume that the Soviet Union will not break up and will not give up its foreign policy of expansion, because the present pattern of American relations with Western Europe, Canada, Japan, and China depends in large part on the scale and momentum of Soviet expansion. The magnitude and persistence of the Soviet thrust for dominion forces nations desiring to remain independent to seek American protective power, and especially the protective power of the American nuclear arsenal.

Equally, the United States will continue to realize, I assume and hope, that it will remain capable of achieving a balance of world power essential to its own independence if but only if it collaborates with Western Europe, Canada, Japan, China, and many smaller nations which share a mutual interest in independence. At the level of instinct, if not of theory, the United States has always understood that the control of the Eurasian land mass by a single power would be fatal to its security. Our supreme national security interest is to make sure that no such development takes place. During this century we have therefore fought at least five wars in the Atlantic and the Pacific Basins, and played a leading role in the formation and development of NATO and other security arrangements, to keep first Germany and Japan, and now the Soviet Union, from achieving mastery. To the same end, we have given the Soviet Union a nuclear warning to deter a Soviet attack on China.

If the major premise for American security planning is that the Soviet Union will not break up or alter its character, my second political assumption follows. Despite the tensions and frictions natural to the life of an alliance, we must assume that the centripetal forces will continue to be stronger than the centrifugal, and that neither we nor our allies will indulge our frustrations and irritations, however tempted we may be. Therefore, by the year 2010, we should still be preoccupied with the Cold War as it has evolved since 1945—or 1917—whichever date you prefer.

The Cold War will surely change somewhat around the edges: slowly and reluctantly the Western nations will move to a more active defense, if only because the Soviet Union's policies of expansion exceed the limits of Western tolerance. The Truman Doctrine was announced to prevent Soviet takeovers in Greece and Turkey. In recent years, we have been hesitating about Soviet moves to enlarge its bridgehead in Cuba—a bridgehead President Eisenhower should never have permitted.

In the meantime, the Western nations are unwillingly being forced to reexamine George Kennan's 1947 thesis, which has been the predicate of Western policy toward the Soviet Union ever since—the thesis, namely, that 10 or 15 years of containment and the benign influence of Russian high culture would mellow the Soviet thrust for power, and persuade the Soviet Union to live within its own legitimate borders in accordance with the rules of international law. Obviously, George Kennan's prediction has not come true, nor can we predicate policy on the assumption that it will come true before the year 2010. We must assume the Soviet Union will not mellow under the influence of the moral code of Russian culture alone.

Let us assume, however, that while the West might well pursue a strategy of cautious and well-considered counterattack, such efforts will not escalate into general war. I suggest such a hypothesis for two reasons: first, the restraining influence of the nuclear balance, provided we restore that balance decisively; second, the relationship between the Soviet government and the Soviet people. The Soviet leadership vividly remembers that in 1956 Soviet troops deserted and fought with the Hungarian rebels in the streets of Budapest and other Hungarian cities. In 1968 the Soviets used Asiatic troops to invade Czechoslovakia and pulled them out after a couple of days to avoid the risk of contamination.

In short, then, nuclear deterrence will still be a relevant issue in 2010, and indeed it is the first issue we have to face in trying to answer the question of how secure we shall feel 22 years from now.

Nuclear Deterrence

I shall not pause long to consider what nuclear arsenals we are supposed to deter. When we had a nuclear monopoly, we thought that one waggle of our nuclear finger would stop aggression anywhere—small or large, nuclear or non-nuclear. Our nuclear monopoly had no such effect, however. It had an effect on some political decisions but not that effect. True, a certain number of military or para-military campaigns were stopped, thanks to explicit or implicit nuclear warnings—the Cuban missile crisis, the Korean War, the Berlin Airlift, and a few others. But many conventional uses of force against our interests occurred—some at very high cost—like those in Korea and Vietnam. How many wars and near wars were prevented because of implicit or explicit nuclear threats is a more difficult question. Surely the failure of the Soviet Union to attack Western Europe or Japan directly is due in considerable part to our nuclear strength and political commitments. Similarly, President Nixon's warning to the Soviet Union probably deterred a Soviet attack on China's nuclear plants in 1969 or 1970.

Today, more than 40 years into the nuclear age, it is apparent that the United States and the Soviet Union have completely different doctrines about the use of nuclear forces, and therefore completely different approaches to the problem of arms control agreements for nuclear weapons.

The United States nuclear posture is designed to deter any Soviet attacks, conventional or nuclear, on the United States and its most vital interests abroad—its allies, its forces stationed abroad, or any interests which stand in the way of Soviet expansion. In a nuclear environment constantly changing under the influence of changes in technology and the Soviet building program, the goal of American nuclear policy is to retain at all times an unquestionable capacity to retaliate if such interests are threatened. Such a retaliatory capacity, we assume, would deter attacks of this order. American policy in the nuclear arms control negotiations is therefore to attain agreements based on the principle of Soviet-American equality in deterrent retaliatory capacity. Such agreements theoretically prevent either side from altering the nuclear balance in its favor by executing a preemptive first strike, while allowing each side to protect its vital interests by using a credible threat of nuclear retaliation. It has been and remains the American and Western view that such agreements could stabilize expectations even during crisis and thus reduce the risk of nuclear war.

For a long time, the United States Government assumed that Soviet nuclear policy was the same as our own. And even now, many Western students of the problem have difficulty accepting the fact that the Soviet concept of deterrence is entirely different from ours. But the Soviet buildup of conventional and nuclear arms, the pattern of Soviet expansion since 1945, and the Soviet negotiating posture in the nuclear arms control talks are consistent with only one hypothesis: that the Soviet nuclear policy is to build a force capable of deterring any American response—conventional or nuclear—to Soviet aggression against American security interests. To that end, the Soviets seek a nuclear arsenal overwhelmingly superior to that of the United States, especially in ground-based ballistic missiles—the most destructive, accurate, and speedy of nuclear weapons, and the ones least vulnerable to defensive weapons. Correspondingly, the Soviet objective in the arms control talks is to gain American and Western acquiescence in a Soviet "right" to massive nuclear superiority. The 1972 Interim Agreement on Offensive Weapons recognized a Soviet advantage in ICBMs, and the Soviet Union has been steadily enlarging that differential in the intervening years.

Thus the Soviet and American views of deterrence are completely opposed: The American goal is to deter Soviet *aggression* against our interests; the Soviet, to deter any American *defense* against Soviet aggression.

When the SALT I agreements were signed in 1972, the United States and the Soviet Union had approximately the same number of warheads on intercontinental ground-based ballistic missiles, and the United States had a comfortable lead in sea-based and airborne forces. The American capacity for nuclear retaliation was beyond question. At the present time, despite the SALT limits, the Soviet Union has a lead of more than three-and-a-half to one in the number of warheads on deployed ICBMs, and a lead of more than four to one in the throw-weight of these weapons. Soviet sea-based and airborne nuclear forces have made comparable though less spectacular gains. In addition, the Soviets have a near monopoly of advanced intermediate range ground-based weapons threatening targets in Europe, Japan, China, and the Middle East. This development occurred during a decade in which shifts in the Soviet-American intercontinental balance raised doubts about the US ability to deter attacks against its security interests most fundamental to the balance of power: the independence of Japan, China, Western Europe, South Korea, and the Middle East.[2]

Why has the Soviet Union been building nuclear weapons at such a frantic rate for so long? The only explanation compatible with its behavior is that it views nuclear weapons as a political rather than a military force. Any dispassionate study of the negotiations against the background of events suggests the hypothesis that the Soviet Union is trying to achieve a plausible first-strike capacity—not in order to fight a nuclear war but to achieve victory without war. The Soviets want to separate the United States from its allies both in the Atlantic and the Pacific and force it into a posture of neutrality and isolation. Faced with a Soviet first-strike capacity, they believe the United States and the Western nations generally would be unable to use conventional force in self defense if the Soviet Union were willing to threaten maximum violence.

Henry Kissinger once asked, "What on earth can one do with nuclear superiority"? The Soviet answer to his question is quite obvious. The Soviet Union believes that clear-cut nuclear superiority would be the ultimate sanction behind its program of indefinite expansion achieved by conventional means, proxy forces, terror, and insurrection aided from abroad. DeGaulle, Kissinger, and Nixon have confirmed such a view of Soviet policy with their remarks to the effect that no Great Power commits suicide in order to protect an ally.

Thus little real danger of nuclear war exists, at least among the industrialized states. Why should the Soviet Union plunge into the unknown by firing a nuclear weapon when its nuclear arms buildup has such a corrosive political effect on Western policy? To recall Raymond Aron's paraphrase of Clausewitz, the Soviet Union has reversed Clausewitz; for the Soviets, politics is a continuation of war by other means.

In this respect, Soviet nuclear strategy echoes the strategy of Germany in building its high seas fleet before 1914. The German objective was not to fight the Royal Navy but to force Great Britain to remain neutral in the event of a general war on the continent of Europe. Soviet strategists believe a clear-cut Soviet first-strike capability would lead the United States to withdraw its forces from Europe, the Mediterranean, and the Far East and adopt a policy of neutrality in the event of an attack on American allies or other American interests. The revolutionary implications of such a change in the magnetic field of world power are the central problem in the minds of responsible officials throughout the world.

Against this background, the rapidly growing force of Soviet intermediate-range ground-based missiles intensifies the pressures which tend to divide the United States from its allies. Intermediate weapons are not a separate military category because, after all,

ICBMs do not have to be fired to the full limit of their radius. ICBMs threaten Western Europe, China, Japan, and the Middle East as much as they threaten targets in the United States. The NATO allies recognized this Soviet strategy when they made their two-track decision in 1979, and experienced the robust Soviet campaign to reverse that decision between 1981 and 1983. The paragraph in the 1985 Geneva Summit Communique—committing the United States and the Soviet Union to seek an interim agreement abolishing intermediate range nuclear weapons—highlights the true purpose of Soviet nuclear policy. Without accompanying agreements on intercontinental offensive weapons and on defensive weapons as well, an agreement abolishing intermediate-range weapons could only increase the nuclear pressure on Western Europe, China, and Japan, and reduce the credibility of the threat of an American response. Giving up the SS-20 would be a cheap price for the Soviet Union to pay for such a result.

The pressures emanating from the Soviet-American nuclear balance are palpable in the politics of all the Western countries. Helmut Schmidt has talked about the "subliminal" influence of the nuclear weapon. The prospect that the Soviets could destroy most of the American retaliatory force with just 25 or 30 percent of their ICBMs fosters the mirage of isolation, neutrality, and accommodation. No one in the West has the slightest desire to discover whether the arcane calculations of a Soviet first-strike capability would prove accurate if put to the test.

As the Scowcroft Commission pointed out in 1983, "The Soviets ... now probably possess the necessary combination of ICBM numbers, reliability, accuracy, and warhead yield to destroy almost all of the 1,047 US ICBM silos, using only a portion of their own ICBM force."[3] A Soviet first-strike capability is implicit in this scenario— the Soviet ability to destroy our ICBM force, our planes on the ground, and our submarines in port, using less than one-third of its ICBM force. When the Soviet

Union's near monopoly of intermediate-range ground-based ballistic missiles is added in, the US position becomes even worse. The plain fact is that the Soviets can now destroy a range of hardened military targets and we cannot. This "one-sided strategic advantage" in ground-based ballistic missiles, the Scowcroft Commission Report said, "casts a shadow over the calculus of Soviet risk taking at every level of confrontation with the West."[4] We cannot safely permit that imbalance to continue; it must "be redressed promptly," the Scowcroft Commission concluded.[5] No President of the United States should ever be confronted with the choice between nuclear war or abandoning vital national security interests.

A Soviet first-strike capability lies at the heart of the Soviet plan to separate the United States from its allies in Europe, Asia, and the Middle East by means of political pressure. Stability, predictability, and deterrence cannot be restored until the Soviet first-strike capability is eliminated.

There are only three ways for achieving that goal:

1. A crash American building program: MX, Midgetman, cruise missiles, Pershing II, and others.

2. The development of defensive weapons which might transform the nuclear equation by requiring the Soviets to use 80 percent or 90 percent of their nuclear force in a first strike rather than 25 or 30 percent.

3. An arms agreement with the Soviet Union based on the principle of Soviet-American deterrent retaliatory equality—the only kind of arms agreement which might allow America to prevent Soviet nuclear blackmail, and the only kind of arms agreement the Western nations should consider.

The sole significant difference between the Soviet Union and the United States during the last 20 years of nuclear arms talks has concerned this crucial issue— Soviet-American equality. The United States has pressed for agreements based on this principle; the Soviets have

adamantly refused, holding out for what they call
"equality and equal security," an Aesopian phrase
which would entitle them to a force equal to the sum of
all the other nuclear forces in the world. To put the
matter bluntly, the Soviet goal in the negotiations has
been to induce the United States to acknowledge the
Soviet Union's "right" to nuclear superiority. That is
why they have pressed for the inclusion of British and
French forces in the agreement, although they know
that those forces are no threat to the far superior Soviet
arsenal, but exist for quite different national purposes.
To date the Soviets have held out for agreements based
on the principle of equal reduction, *not* reduction to
equal levels, which was the basis for the 1922 Washington Naval Agreements. This Soviet approach would
make the crucial Soviet advantage in ground-based
ballistic missiles even bigger and more intimidating than
it is now.

The Nuclear Balance and SDI

The United States has little time to restore the
nuclear balance on which the possibility of our having a
foreign policy depends. One of the most promising
ways to seek that goal is to explore defensive technologies which might significantly diminish the capabilities of the Soviet missile force. Such is the purpose
of the Strategic Defense Initiative (SDI) announced by
President Reagan in 1983.

President Reagan's Strategic Defense Initiative is a
carefully considered and intellectually sound attempt to
escape from the terrible dilemma of strictly offensive
nuclear deterrence. Deterrence through the threat of
nuclear annihilation has always been morally abhorrent.
In fact, SDI is the most idealistic nuclear initiative since
the Baruch Plan President Truman proposed in 1946. It
promises a practical way to help overcome the deterio-
ration in the strategic balance in offensive weapons

which we foolishly allowed to take place after the 1972 SALT I agreements.

SDI bristles with difficult problems for both Americans and their allies and adversaries; it will take time, patience, and extended analysis and consultation to resolve our positions constructively. In addition, like every other major technological revolution, SDI has stirred up a flurry of resistance among those who resent any change to our comfortable and familiar universe of thought.

The first thing I should say about SDI is that it is misnamed. As Professor Edward Teller has pointed out, it should have been called the Strategic Defense *Response*, because the Soviet Union has spent more money on strategic defense since 1972—when the ABM Treaty was signed and ratified—than on offensive nuclear weapons. On the contrary, the United States has done minimal research in the field since 1972 and has fallen far behind the Soviet Union. President Reagan's decision to accelerate our SDI research program was therefore inevitable—like President Franklin Roosevelt's decision to build an atomic bomb after a group of scientists told him that Hitler was already attempting to do so. If the Soviet Union achieves the only significant nuclear defensive capability in the world, the nuclear balance will tip even further against us, and the balance of power will be in mortal peril as a consequence.

Second, as the Administration fully recognizes, the full potentialities of SDI will take years to realize, even if the US research effort should prove successful. For the indefinite future, we should consider defensive weapons within our present framework of deterrence through the threat of retaliation. In this perspective, SDI is a partial alternative to a massive buildup of offensive weapons to restore and reinforce our policy of deterrence. As Ambassador Nitze has said,

The present situation—in which the threat of massive nuclear retaliation is the ultimate sanction, the
key element of deterrence, and thus the basis for
security and peace—is unsatisfactory. It has kept
the peace for 40 years, but the potential costs of a
breakdown are immense and, because of continuing massive Soviet deployments of both offensive
and defensive weaponry, are not becoming less. If
we can, we must find a more reliable basis for
security and for peace.

This concern prompted the President's decision to
proceed with the Strategic Defense Initiative. He
has directed the scientific community to determine
if new cost-effective defensive technologies are feasible that could be introduced into force structures
so as to produce a more stable strategic relationship. We envisage, if that search is successful, a
cooperative effort with the Soviet Union, hopefully
leading to an agreed transition towards effective
non-nuclear defenses that might make possible the
eventual elimination of nuclear weapons.[6]

Thus, between now and 2010 the strategic problem
is exactly the same as that during the negotiation of
SALT I: to achieve nuclear stability by stabilizing the
relationship between offensive and defensive arms. In
the early 1970s, the primary Soviet concern was to suppress what they thought was an American lead in anti-
ballistic missiles (ABMs). The Soviet Union accepted the
Five-Year Interim Agreement on Offensive Weapons of
1972 only when the United States made it clear that it
would not agree to the ABM Treaty without the Interim
Agreement. Even when the Interim Agreement was
signed, the US issued a formal statement, declaring that
its supreme security interests could be engaged if the
Soviet Union failed to agree to the permanent regula-
tion of offensive weapons. In such an event, we said,
the ABM Treaty might be abrogated.

The literature on ballistic missile defenses is enormous and somewhat repetitive, though a few key issues
deserve discussion.

First, is there a significant difference between deterrence through the threat of retaliation and deterrence through defensive weapons? I do not think so. It is hard to imagine why a nuclear defensive shield over the industrialized democracies, however efficient, would deter a Soviet attack on the Persian Gulf or South Korea. To deter such an attack, or to defeat it with conventional force, requires a capacity to retaliate against the Soviet Union with nuclear weapons.

As I have argued earlier, the key instrument of aggression, so far as nuclear weapons are concerned, is a visible and plausible first-strike capability. That certainly seems to be the Soviet view. Effective nuclear defenses would fundamentally alter the nuclear equation: it could take 80 or 90 percent rather than 25 or 30 percent of the Soviet ICBM force to knock out the bulk of our nuclear arsenal. Such a transformation would greatly reduce nuclear fear and the possibility of Soviet nuclear blackmail. It would also diminish the appeal of illusions like isolationism in the United States and of accommodation in Europe and Japan.

Under these circumstances, the US threat of a retaliatory nuclear strike against a Soviet conventional or nuclear force attack on our allies or our overseas interests would once again become convincing—that is, we would recover our deterrent influence and be able to use conventional weapons with increased confidence.

Would this perspective change if Soviet nuclear defenses were at least as good as ours? Yes, but only in one way. A Soviet and American standoff in defensive weapons would produce nuclear stalemate between the Soviet Union and the United States and areas of the world protected by American nuclear defenses. Though both sides would notably have some retaliatory capacity, neither side would have a first-strike capacity. Under such circumstances, the United States and its allies could use conventional forces to defend their interests. This would not be the case if we permit the Soviet Union to maintain a first-strike capability.

A world of perfectly effective anti-nuclear astro-domes would present different problems for Western policy, but such a world lies well beyond 2010.

A second key issue mentioned in SDI literature is really the next step in the analysis I have just begun: if successfully deployed, would SDI make "extended deterrence" impossible? I do not think so.

Our allies are gravely and legitimately concerned about SDI. They cannot help wondering whether the United States is seeking to immunize itself from the nuclear plague, and whether effective American ballistic missile defenses would make the American nuclear umbrella incredible as a protection for any American interests beyond the territories of the United States. As I indicated earlier in another connection, a moderately successful SDI should have precisely the opposite effect. It would help to annul the Soviet Union's present nuclear advantage in ground-based intercontinental and intermediate-range missiles, thus restoring the diminishing credibility of America's promise to retaliate with nuclear weapons if Soviet aggression is directed against vital American interests abroad. Our allies' fear is natural; it should be taken seriously, and I believe the Reagan Administration is taking it seriously, both through extended consultations and through its offer to make the entire SDI program a cooperative venture.

Exactly the same anxiety has been a weapon of American isolationists hoping for a way to escape from the tribulations of the real world. They argue that since our security commitments to NATO could involve us in overseas war with nuclear overtones, we should abandon our commitments and conduct a foreign policy of "unilateral internationalism," thus freeing us from the tiresome burden of managing alliances. However, given the arithmetic of world power, any unilateral American effort to protect our national interest in the balance of power would be doomed to failure. We could never achieve the military capacity to do so.

Another Allied concern is whether SDI would reduce the significance of the independent British and French nuclear forces, or the emergence of Europe as a nuclear political entity. The British and the French—and many other Europeans as well—are concerned about the development of Soviet ballistic missile defenses which could weaken the deterrent influence of the small European forces. Such a concern would be justified only if the United States and the Soviet Union were both protected by nuclear defenses.

However, if SDI becomes a cooperative project involving most of our allies, the resulting defenses should enhance British and French deterrence, as well as that of the United States. At the present time, the credibility of the British and French forces is low against those of the Soviet Union because of their numerical disparity. Any defensive measures which lessen the first-strike capability of the Soviets against the United States can only increase the credibility of British and French forces. A successful cooperative Allied SDI program is one way of achieving such a goal.

President Reagan has been ridiculed for proposing to cooperate with the Soviet Union in suppressing nuclear weapons altogether. I for one strongly support President Reagan's proposal, however Utopian it may seem today. The nuclear arms race has become an insanity, threatening civilization itself. Only cooperative efforts involving the two nuclear superpowers and the other key nations of the world can stop the madness. The hope behind SDI is that emerging defense technology will convince the Soviet leaders that the nuclear equation has become so complex, and contains so many and such mysterious variables, that it can be brought under control only by the joint efforts of the Soviet Union and the United States—indeed of all the major powers ultimately.

A corollary of this thesis should be carefully noted. Cooperative methods for balancing the nuclear equation demand that the Soviets abide by the rules of the

Charter of the United Nations regarding the international use of force. There is no use in having even a good agreement about nuclear arms if its main effect would be to make the world safe for Soviet aggression achieved by the use of non-nuclear forces.

Some SDI analysts question whether developing Soviet and American defenses would drive nuclear deterrence back to Mutual Assured Destruction. This question is important and difficult to answer, especially as we examine the cost effectiveness of various alternatives offered by the emerging technologies. The dilemma these analysts pose cannot be avoided. But the dilemma would become even worse if the United States allowed the Soviet Union a free field in developing, testing, and deploying ballistic missile defenses. The problem is one of many created by the implacable development of technology. It cannot be solved unilaterally.

The problem of extended deterrence is not a matter of technology and the nuclear balance alone, but of psychology and feeling. It is also our most important and most difficult security problem. Almost everyone writing about extended deterrence takes it for granted that effective ballistic missile defenses in the United States would make us less willing to risk nuclear war to prevent the Soviet conquest of Japan or Western Europe. For example, Keith Payne and Colin Gray say, "A defensive deterrent would ... present powerful disincentives against a Soviet nuclear first strike. It is likely, however, to be less appropriate for the current policy of extending deterrence coverage to allies and global interests."[7] The only remedy for that development, Payne and Gray conclude, is enhanced conventional force defenses. The difficulty with this argument, however, is that without a genuine American nuclear retaliatory capacity, conventional force defenses for Europe, Japan, or other American global interests cannot be used. That was the lesson the Soviet Union learned during the Cuban missile crisis of 1962. We could have invaded Cuba at will with conventional forces because of our nuclear superiority. Therefore, the Soviets withdrew.

However, if our foremost national security interest is to prevent any one power from dominating the Eurasian-African land mass—and it is—then we must solve the problem. How can it be solved? How can we defend our most basic security interests without nuclear war?

The answer lies, I suggest, not through larger conventional forces alone, as some have suggested, but through a decisively restored nuclear balance. Once that is done, our nuclear retaliatory capability could serve the same constructive role it has played in shaping the world between 1945 and the late 1960s—that is, by preventing direct and indirect Soviet attacks on the key components of the world power structure, and forcing the Soviets to pursue their strategic goal in costly, prolonged, ambiguous, and ultimately futile struggles in the Third World, some of which in fact were terminated by American nuclear threats.

There is no way to escape from this imperative. Conventional forces alone can never be the answer. As Robert McNamara conceded during the debate over the "no-first-use" issue, we can never be sure the Soviet Union would *not* use nuclear weapons first. Consequently, we must retain a persuasive retaliatory capability even if we adopt a "no-first-use" policy. Payne and Gray suggest the same point in their 1984 *Foreign Affairs* article: "[I]f America is defended, the President is likely to see a lower level of risk involved in responding to a Soviet invasion of Europe than if America were naked to Soviet nuclear attack. This fact alone should significantly reduce any Soviet inclination to attack NATO Europe."[8] Payne and Gray assume that the American response under such circumstances would be largely or entirely conventional. But for many years to come, the key issue will be to maintain our nuclear retaliatory capacity. We could never fight a prolonged conventional war in Europe or elsewhere unless we had the backing of a nuclear retaliatory capability. Unless the Soviet Union achieves a perfect nuclear astrodome, it could never imagine it could make nuclear threats with complete immunity.

There is in fact an even more paradoxical dimension to the nuclear dilemma. We need exactly the same nuclear arsenal to deter a direct attack against the United States and an attack against an ally or another vital interest overseas. In order to be able to use conventional weapons in the defense of Long Island, Alaska, or Japan, we must have exactly the same nuclear retaliatory capacity. In other words, there is no difference between "deterrence" and "extended deterrence"—between defending the homeland and defending our national security interests overseas. If the Soviet Union had overwhelming nuclear superiority and threatened to land in the United States, would we fight on the beaches, or would we do what the Soviets did during the Cuban Missile Crisis in 1962, when President Kennedy called Khrushchev's bluff? Of course, we should be extremely angry if the Soviet Union made any such threat against the United States. We would be even more furious if they underlined their seriousness by a nuclear demonstration—destroying our satellites, or blowing up an American city, for example. Under such circumstances, our instinct would be to strike back, to do something. But would the President really kill 10 million Soviet citizens in his rage, knowing that 50 million Americans would be killed an hour later?

Obviously, neither the American public nor Congress has yet absorbed this fundamental lesson of the Cuban missile crisis. The inarticulate premise behind the willingness of so many members of Congress to vote for defense cuts is surely the notion that "whatever happens, we have enough to keep them off Long Island, and the rest of the world doesn't really matter after all." The brutal fact, however, is that if the US cannot keep the Soviets out of Tokyo, Paris, or Rome, it doesn't have enough to keep them off Hawaii either.

Conclusion

If the assumptions on which I have based my analysis are reasonable, then my conclusion is simple. Despite the complications introduced by the nuclear weapon and other transformations brought about by high-technology, the nature of world politics has not changed. Its problems would have been familiar to Thucydides, when war was carried on with spears, swords, and arrows, and warships were rowed by men. Nuclear weapons make nuclear war unlikely, though not impossible, especially if weapons continue to become smaller, cleaner, and more accurate. But the nuclear weapon does not make conventional war, proxy war, limited war, or irregular war carried out by subversion, propaganda, and terrorism less likely—except between major nuclear powers, since the possibility of escalation from conventional war is a wild card. The successful development of ballistic missile defenses should make it easier for us to eliminate the threat of a Soviet first-strike capability even if Soviet progress in the field matches our own. On that footing—and only on that footing—will it be possible for the West to restore the vitality of collective security in the Atlantic, the Pacific, and the Middle East.

If we succeed in this effort, and if we convince the Soviet leadership that we will never again allow the nuclear balance to tip against us as we did in the 1970s and early 1980s, then stabilizing nuclear arms agreements may well become feasible. To be stabilizing, such agreements would have to regulate both offensive and defensive weapons, including anti-satellite weapons. It does no good to bridge half a river, as Dean Rusk remarked some years ago. By then, conceivably, the Soviet Union may discover that the quest for empire is a mug's game which the bidder for mastery can never win. If that happens before 2010, we shall all be more secure.

Eugene V. Rostow received his A.B. from Yale University in 1933, studied economics at Kings College, Cambridge, and received an LL.B. from Yale in 1937. In addition to a number of honorary degrees, he was awarded an LL.D. by Cambridge University in 1962 for the quality of his scholarly work.

Dr. Rostow joined the Yale faculty in 1938, and has been a member ever since, with periods of leave for public service and as Visiting Professor in Cambridge (1959-60), Oxford (1970-71), and the University of Chicago (1941). Dr. Rostow became Professor Emeritus and Senior Research Scholar at Yale in 1984. He was Dean of the Yale Law School between 1955 and 1965; Assistant to Dean Acheson when he was Assistant Secretary of State, 1942-44; Assistant to the Executive Secretary of the Economic Commission for Europe in 1949-50; Undersecretary of State for Political Affairs, 1966-69; and Director of the Arms Control and Disarmament Agency, 1981-83.

Dr. Rostow has written a number of books and many articles in scholarly and popular journals.

NOTES

1. This paper was given in 1986, and it has recently been reviewed for publication. Have the spectacular events of the last two-and-a-half years altered Soviet foreign policy enough to require a change in the assumption on which the paper rests? Mr. Gorbachev has of course proclaimed a new day, and announced a program of peace. But thus far his actions do not confirm his words. No one in the West can be confident that the Soviet Union has in fact abandoned the strategy of expansion to which the Western policy of containment is a response. Soviet military budgets continue to grow, and more growth is projected for the future. The Soviet Union had modified, perhaps even given up a number of its Third World campaigns which were proved disappointing or counterproductive, but it continues others with energy, and it has greatly intensified its long-standing effort to denuclearize and neutralize Western Europe and detach it from NATO. The political pressure of nuclear and conventional force superiority is the key weapon in its effort to achieve this end, which has been the primary strategic objective of its foreign policy since 1945. Under these circumstances, the West must treat Gorbachev's innovations in foreign policy as tactical and not strategic, and view the INF Treaty, at least until the entire Soviet American Nuclear equation is stabilized, as decoupling.

2. Since this chapter was written, of course, the INF Treaty was signed and ratified. It calls for the abolition of intermediate range ground-based nuclear weapons, by both the Soviet Union and the United States. The Soviet Union has deployed some four times as many weapons in this category as the United States. The effect of the INF Treaty on the Soviet-American nuclear equation remains ambiguous, however, since all the targets in Europe, Japan, China, and the United States threatened by the weapons to be abolished under the INF Treaty can be reached also by redundant Soviet longer-range offensive weapons. It will not be possible to evaluate the significance of INF until agreements based on the principle of equality are reached on the other two elements in the nuclear equation: offensive weapons and defensive systems. In the absence of such agreements, the effect of INF will be somewhat (but not decisively) "decoupling"—that is, it will

tend to separate Western Europe, China, Japan, and other United States interests from the United States by making the American nuclear guarantee less credible.

3. *Report of the President's Commission on Strategic Forces,* April 1983, p. 4.

4. Ibid., p. 5.

5. Ibid., p. 6

6. Paul H. Nitze, "On the Road to a More Stable Peace," February 20, 1985 in *Essays on Strategy and Diplomacy* (Claremont, CA: The Keck Center for International Strategic Studies, May 1985), p. 33.

7. Keith B. Payne and Colin S. Gray, "Nuclear Policy and the Defensive Transition, *Foreign Affairs* (Spring 1984), p. 829.

8. Ibid., p. 831.

INDEX

Security Implications of SDI

Composed with text and display type in Optima
Cover art and illustrations prepared by Jim Price
Book design by Donald Schmoldt

Special Credits
NDU Press Editor: Donald Schmoldt
Editorial Reader: Dr. William McCarron
Editorial Clerks: Pat Williams and Myrna Morgan

105544

UG
743
.S43
1990

Security
implications of
SDI.

DATE DUE

GAYLORD

PRINTED IN U.S.A.

YOU CAN
Speak Up in Class

YOU CAN
Speak Up in Class

SARA GILBERT
illustrated by ROY DOTY

MORROW JUNIOR BOOKS   NEW YORK

Text copyright © 1991 by Sara Gilbert

Illustrations copyright © 1991 by Roy Doty

Printed in the United States of America.
1 2 3 4 5 6 7 8 9 10

Library of Congress Cataloging-in-Publication Data
Gilbert, Sara D.
You can speak up in class / Sara Gilbert ; illustrated by Roy Doty.
p. cm. Includes index.
Summary: Discusses the different aspects of being uncomfortable or
afraid when speaking in the classroom, the reasons for such
problems, and ways of dealing with them effectively.
ISBN 0-688-09867-3 (lib. bdg.).—ISBN 0-688-10304-9 (pbk.)
1. Oral communication—Juvenile literature. 2. Language arts
(Elementary)—Juvenile literature. [1. Oral communication.
2. Communication.] I. Doty, Roy, 1922– ill. II. Title.
LB1572.G55 1991
372.6—dc20 90-19268 CIP

For Andrea—
with special thanks

Contents

YOU CAN
Speak Up in Class

What if
you can't speak up in class?

At school, do you ever find that you know the answer to a question but can't seem to get your hand up or the words out? Do you ever feel like joining in the class discussion but don't? Do those feelings get worse when you have to stand in front of the class? Do you ever wish that speaking in class didn't make you nervous?

Well, you *can* speak up in class.

What's so hard about speaking up in class? You just open your mouth and let the words come out, right? Wrong! If speaking up were that simple, it wouldn't scare so many kids (grown-ups, too!). Many people have trouble speaking up in class—volunteering to speak, or answering a teacher's question, or making a report. It can be a serious problem, although many people don't take it seriously.

In this book, you will have a chance to give some serious thought to solving the problem of speaking in public. The *What if* pages in this book talk about all the different ways that speaking up in class is hard. When you read the list of these *What if*'s in the table of contents, you may find that all of the situations apply to you. Or you may feel that only a few are ones that make it hard for *you* to speak up in class. Either way, you may be surprised to learn that the *What if*'s that make you nervous make other people nervous, too.

The *Try this* pages that follow each *What if* problem offer solutions. These sections will help you to *think about* each situation that's tough for you and to figure out why it's hard. They will also give you things *to do*—ideas to explore, words to say, and actions to take—to make each situation easier. In fact, you have already started to try. You have started to read this book and may have even looked at the list of *What if* situations and thought about which ones are toughest for you.

Don't worry! Even though the problems are hard, the solutions are simple. How simple? Keep reading.

What if you had a magic formula to solve your problem? Well, in a way you do. It's even better than magic, because it's a formula that you can use to solve this and any other problem.

It has only three parts.

2

1. Become **AWARE** of what bothers you—"What's the problem?"
2. Figure out your **ATTITUDE** about it—"What are the *facts*?" "How do I really feel about them?" "What am I willing to do to change?"
3. **ACT**—"What do I do?" "What do I do *first*?"

To apply this better-than-magic formula to your speaking-up-in-class problem, you would

1. become **AWARE** of what bothers you by finding the *What if* problems that upset you most
2. figure out your **ATTITUDE** about them by trying the THINK ABOUTs that go with each problem
3. **ACT** by practicing the DO THIS suggestions in each section.

How hard are the actions you have to take? Here's something that may surprise you: There are three (and really only three) ways to solve a problem or resolve a worry:

admit it and do something about it until it goes away

act as if it weren't a worry

do it anyway, even if you think you can't.

And all three solutions work! You can take one approach or combine two or three. Whichever actions you choose, you will solve your problem.

Why not get a piece of paper and a pencil and write the formula down: AWARE—ATTITUDE—ACT: ADMIT—ACT AS IF—DO IT ANYWAY. Then keep the paper handy; you'll need it again soon.

And remember that *Try this* really means *try* it! Say the words, do the exercises, follow the suggestions that you find with each *What if*. Being able to speak up takes practice.

In case this sounds like too much work and you think it's easier not to speak up, ask yourself: What if you don't speak up in class? After all, if you don't, you won't ever make a mistake. Or will you?

What if you have something to say that would impress the teacher or your classmates? If you don't speak up, no one will ever know.

What if you don't care about that? Then remember that part of your grade depends on class participation. So if you don't speak up, you have to do that much better on your other work to get a good grade.

But you can't get good grades if you don't understand the work. If you don't speak up, you might make a mistake on your homework or on a test. What if you need help? If you don't speak up, you might never catch up.

If you don't speak up in class, the teacher and your classmates won't pay attention to you. "That's just fine," you might say. "I don't want anyone to notice me."

But you are concerned about speaking up in class, aren't you? It feels like a problem, doesn't it? Maybe it's not the worst problem in the world, but it is one that you will be better off without.

Why? Well, think about your classmates who don't speak up, either. What kind of impression do they make on you? Do they seem stupid? Do they do silly things to get attention? Are they tough characters you wouldn't want to bother? Or are they scared little mice you don't want to bother with? Whatever impression those kids make on you is how *you* seem to others when you don't speak up in class! Is that how you want to seem? (Your teacher might not even think you were there at all!) Something to think about. . . .

Now, think again—about the kids who *do* speak up. Chances are they are the ones who get better grades, make a good impression on you and others, feel better about themselves, have an easier time in school. This isn't because they're smarter or better but because they can speak up—and you can, too, and can benefit from it like they have.

But what if you feel, "Who cares? I just don't want to do it!"

When people express an attitude like this, especially about something that will help them, what they're often really saying is, "I don't know how" or "I'm afraid to."

If you want to benefit from speaking up in class like those other students do, it hardly makes sense to say, "I don't want to," does it? So if what you really mean is, "I don't know how," then remember that you can *learn* how. This book will show you.

On the other hand, what you may really mean is, "I'm afraid to." Sure, nobody likes to admit to being afraid. Somehow, it seems that admitting fear will make it worse. But that's not always true. Remember the first suggestion for solving a problem or getting rid of a worry: to admit it and do something about it. We often think that only a sissy is afraid. But think about this: Fear is a natural, and important, reaction to situations we don't like. It is the feeling that protects us from danger. And there is probably some good reason why we are afraid. Some people, for instance, have families that don't give them a chance to talk, or criticize everything they say, or just don't listen. Others have had bad experiences in class, with a particular teacher, or in a given subject. Some have had "friends" who teased them.

Try to think of some event in your past that might make you afraid to speak in class. Just brainstorm; let your mind wander freely. Jot down anything that comes to it. You'll find that once you start to understand something about why you (and lots of others) have the fear, you begin putting the problem behind you.

Now check the table of contents, turn to your speaking-up problem—and start. Taking action *today* will begin to solve it!

5

What if
you want to raise your hand?

Everybody knows that raising your hand is easy—right? But it *isn't* easy for everybody. It's hard for a *lot* of people.

If it's hard for you, too, this section will make it easier.

7

What if
you think you're the only one who can't speak up?

Well, you're not. Even though you and everybody else who gets nervous about talking may believe that everybody *else* can do it easily, the truth is that even famous people like politicians, performers, and broadcasters—people who should be used to it—get nervous about talking in public.

You can prove to yourself that people in *your* life have trouble speaking up some of the time.

> You've already noticed the other kids in your class who don't speak up, so you know that there are at least a few people like you.

> Pay attention to those who *do* speak up and you'll probably see that the ones who raise their hands first sometimes freeze up when the teacher *calls on* them, and that even the best talkers look and sound nervous when they have to stand in front of the class.

> Watch the people around you—in class, at home, on the bus, even on TV—and you'll hear them make comments and nervous jokes about just the same things that keep you from speaking up.

Listen, and you'll begin to get the idea that you're *not* the only one who can't speak up. Then . . .

Try this:

THINK ABOUT another strange-but-true idea: The fact that you aren't the only one who gets nervous about speaking almost magically makes it easier to do!

Aren't you already feeling a little better just noticing that other people might have the same problem?

DO THIS: Ask a few people you feel comfortable with—parent, grandparent, aunt, uncle, sister or brother, friend, or teacher— "Did you ever get nervous when you had to talk in class (or make a speech or a report, or make phone calls to people you don't know, or talk to strangers at a party)?" If they say no, try to make them tell the truth! (Surveys show that these situations make *everyone* tense.) At least ask, "How come? What do you do to make it easy?" If they say yes, which is more likely, then ask, "Well, what did you do about it?"

Adults may tell you that speaking up still causes them discomfort—and you'll know why *you* need to find a solution now. Or they may give you some tips you can use.

At the very least, you'll discover that just letting the worry come out of your mouth takes away some of its power, so you can focus on the details of the problem.

What if
you think the other kids will laugh at you?

It's all very well to talk with people you trust, but you know how kids make fun of people. Maybe you've even been laughed at yourself, and it's not a good feeling at all!

Why do kids laugh? Why do people make fun of other people? Often, it's because *they* feel uncomfortable about something.

> If they can find something wrong with you, it makes them feel less is "wrong" about themselves.

> If they point out something laughable about you, they keep attention away from themselves.

> If they can laugh with a group at someone outside the group, they feel somehow safer.

Or they may laugh with relief that they aren't the ones (at least for now) who can't answer the question or get the words out.

Even if you understand all that, being made to feel like a fool or the butt of a joke is still very uncomfortable. Nobody likes it. But you will be letting those people have the last laugh if you shut up and try to disappear. So . . .

Try this:

THINK ABOUT the worst thing that can happen if you get laughed at: Will you die? Will you have to quit school or leave town? No. If you're really honest with yourself, you'll see that the worst that can happen is . . . you'll get laughed at! Compare that "worst" with the list on page 4 of what can happen if you don't speak up at all.

Now, imagine yourself volunteering to speak . . . being called on . . . standing at the front of the class . . . and doing or saying something that makes people laugh.

And imagine how you will react if that happens: Will you run out of the room? Start to cry? Throw a tantrum? Attack the teasers? Or laugh back?

Which is the reaction least likely to cause more trouble? Think about it: If someone is teasing you, you take away his or her nasty power if you laugh along.

DO THIS: Pick one or two people in your class whom you admire or envy. Observe them for a while and watch what they do when they are teased. They probably don't fight back or slink away in shame. Probably they join in the laughter at themselves. By doing this, they admit they've made a funny mistake, they act as if it doesn't matter, and they probably go right on. Listen to famous comedians on TV and take note of how many of their jokes are directed at themselves!

So practice laughing at yourself. Make up some jokes about your own flaws. Get ready to laugh if you get laughed at—and you may well find yourself part of the group that's having the fun.

What if
you just can't stand *any* attention?

For some people, it's not laughter or teasing that bothers them, but *any* kind of attention—even praise.

Does that sound like you? Well, you should know that you aren't the only one who feels that way. And you probably don't need to be told how uncomfortable school can be for people who feel this way.

Go back to page 5 and read again about why it's important to speak up in class. Then try to imagine how it will be if you *always* feel so uncomfortable—not just now, in school, but when you're a grown-up, forever.

If that seems terrible, you may be ready to do something about it now! So . . .

Try this:

THINK ABOUT why you feel this way.

Some people who do feel like this come from a very large family and just aren't used to getting attention.

Others come from families that give attention only for bad things, so attention comes to mean "bad."

Some have families that give them so much attention they can't stand any more—especially because they suspect that they're not really "that good."

Many people carry around a bad secret about themselves that they're afraid attention will reveal—or that makes them feel inside that they don't deserve attention.

Or you may simply not want the other kids to think you're a teacher's pet or too brainy to hang out with.

DO THIS: Let your mind remember what may cause you to feel this way. Then do what you can to put it behind you—because the fact is that you don't have to let past experiences control you today (or into your future). Talk about it if you can. Or write about it. Getting those old feelings out, even on paper, can help get rid of them for good.

Then focus on what you can do *now* to make it better:

You can make up your mind to "act as if" attention doesn't bother you— and the more you do, the less it will.

You can "do it anyway": Make yourself speak up just once, even if you don't want to. Try first in a safe place. Do some attention-getting things that don't involve speaking up—bake cookies for your family or write a story or paint a picture for your teacher—to help you get used to the idea.

And though you may not believe it (yet), say every morning "I *do* deserve attention!"

What if

you have nothing to say that anyone wants to hear?

Oh, dear—poor you! "Poor anyone" who gives this as a reason for not speaking up. It may just be another way to say "I'm afraid to." (Remember how hard that is to say?)

Maybe it comes from some bad experiences of being told to shut up in the past. Or maybe you're just not thinking hard enough about what *is* interesting about you.

In either case, instead of feeling sorry for yourself, you will be better off if you . . .

Try this:

THINK ABOUT what's behind this attitude:

> Do you really feel that way, or is this just an excuse to avoid talking?
> If you suspect that it is an excuse, go back to page 5 and give your
> feelings some more thought.

> Try to remember times when you've been put down in not-nice ways
> and recall how you felt then: pretty bad, probably. The previous two
> *Try this* sections should help you put that past where it belongs.

DO THIS: Take a look at yourself today. Look around your room.
Think about places you've been, things you've done. Then make
a list of what's special about you. For instance, What can you make?
Do you play music? Dance? What groups do you belong to? Come
up with at least twenty items that make you interesting.

Also, make a note, in your mind or on a piece of paper, of some
things that you've recently read in books or magazines, seen on
TV, heard on the news, or heard about in your family. When you're
in school, pay attention to the talk going on around you. You'll
probably find you'll have a chance to talk about some of these
topics.

Read through the newspaper every day. That can sometimes
give you something to contribute to a class discussion. It can
always give you something to ask the teacher questions about.

If you try these tips, pretty soon you'll realize that you do have
something to say. All you have to do is try.

What if
you think you'll make the teacher mad?

Maybe you believe the teacher isn't interested in what you have to say. Maybe you worry that if you say the *wrong* thing, you'll make the teacher mad.

Sometimes it may seem easy to do things that make teachers mad—but speaking up isn't one of those things! Here's what makes teachers mad: students who clown around and cause trouble in class . . . students who talk out of turn or who don't listen . . . students who don't do their homework . . . students who don't seem interested in what is going on in class.

In fact, teachers usually must spend so much time and energy controlling the noisy troublemakers that often they don't have time or energy left over to pay much attention to students who are quiet. They may even assume that students who are quiet, who don't volunteer, or who seem to have trouble answering questions haven't done the work or aren't interested—and that makes them mad.

So if you don't speak up, you won't get into the same kind of trouble as the rough and rowdy bunch does, but you won't make the teacher happy, either. You might even cause trouble for yourself by not getting the kind of help and attention that you deserve and that you need in order to learn.

Remember that teachers have spent a lot of time gathering knowledge and learning how to pass it on. They are in the classroom because they want to help people. What tends to make them mad is students who prevent them from doing that. So . . .

16

Try this:

THINK ABOUT how to make teachers happy instead of worrying about making them mad. You've already gone a long way toward making the teacher happy by spending time and thought on the questions and suggestions in this book. The more you can speak up, the more you will be participating in what the teacher is there to do.

DO THIS: Even if you can't yet bring yourself to join in discussions with the whole class, you can ask the teacher questions before or after class, or during a break.

> Ask for more information about something mentioned in a lesson (pick a topic you really have some interest in!).
>
> Ask for help with specific homework or classwork problems ("I didn't quite get problem five," for instance).
>
> Ask for advice on dealing with your general speaking-up trouble ("What if someone has trouble raising his or her hand?").

Rehearse what you're going to ask beforehand, if you need to.

This kind of private speaking up can have several good results. It gives the teacher the idea that you are interested, even though you're quiet. It helps the teacher get to know you—and to know that you have trouble speaking up. It gives you talking practice, plus help with schoolwork!

What if
the other students always beat you to it?

Okay—so you've made up your mind to participate. You've gotten yourself all geared up and thought about some topics to contribute. But when you're in class, it seems that even when you have something to say, the other kids all beat you to it.

What to do? Remember that the students who *do* raise their hands have had a lot of *practice* in raising their hands. All you need is a little practice, too. So . . .

Try this:

THINK ABOUT your classmates who seem to have an easier time raising their hands. Are you sure it's easier, or does it just *seem* that way because they do it? Maybe they're just "acting as if," too—and they've practiced getting their hands up faster. You can, too.

DO THIS: Find a place where it's private; then practice raising your hand. Really! See which hand is more comfortable to raise, your right or your left. Does your hand seem to want to go straight up, or just up from the elbow? Are your fingers open or closed? Do it the easiest way, but exercise that arm again and again in private. Then it will be used to going up in public.

You can rehearse while you're in class, too. Just as you play along with the contestants on a TV game show, for a week in class, each time the teacher asks a question, answer it in your mind as fast as you can. During a class discussion or activity, "say" your piece in your mind and see how long it takes for someone to say that out loud. Then, after a week, start getting your hand up and saying some of those things out loud yourself.

What if
you're just bored?

Maybe you don't want to participate because it's just not interesting enough.

Now, that attitude—like the "I don't care" claim—might just be another way of saying "I'm afraid." If that's the case, reread page 5 to try and figure out why you're afraid.

Or it might be because you've gotten behind and have no idea of what's going on. If you think that might be true, then it's time to ask for help (see page 17).

Often, though, school *is* boring. You have to go, and sit, and behave, when you would really rather be doing something else. Or a particular teacher might be boring—at least to you. Or one subject may be boring to you, and not because it's too hard, but because it's too easy or because you are just not interested in it.

Not all of life is fun and exciting. But there are ways to make it a little more interesting. So . . .

Try this:

THINK ABOUT speaking up rather than just sitting there. Time passes faster when you're involved, so the more you're able to participate in class, the less boring it will be.

DO THIS: Make a list of the things you enjoy doing or want to do. (Or look at the suggestions on page 15.) Pick at least five items to tie to what's going on at school. For instance . . .

use a hobby as the basis for a paper you're assigned

use examples from your after-school job to understand your math homework, or words from games or books you enjoy for spelling and English assignments

instead of waiting to be assigned a project or a report, suggest to the teacher something that *you're* interested in researching and presenting

you might even think of a project the whole class can participate in— a show, a food or clothing drive, a recycling project, or a letter-writing campaign.

You'll see how easy it is to speak up when you're interested— and how fast school gets unboring.

What if
simply talking is hard for you?

For some people, it's not the topics that cause the trouble, it is talking about them that causes problems. Speech itself is complicated. To say even a simple sentence to yourself or your best friend, you call on your mind, your senses, your mouth and lungs, your memory of almost everything you've ever learned, and your feelings about what you are saying. Quite a task!

Some people have special problems with this complex activity. English may not be their native language, and they have difficulty pronouncing some words and putting them together. This can be especially hard if their family speaks another language at home.

They may have a hearing problem or physical trouble with speech that keeps them from getting the words out. (Three *million* grade-school students have some kind of speech problem!)

Vision problems can make speaking up hard, too: If you can't see well, you may not know what you're supposed to be talking about. Or things may look so blurry that you feel disconnected.

Other learning difficulties that have nothing to do with being "smart" or "stupid" can also interfere with a person's ability to learn.

Problems like these can indeed be serious, but they can also be corrected. And they should be—not just to help you speak up but to help you learn more easily. So, if you think that you may have some special difficulty with speech . . .

Try this:

THINK ABOUT how your communications skills compare with those of your classmates.

> Do you seem to have more trouble with your speech, vision, or hearing than the other kids?
>
> Do you read a sentence in a different way from the way your classmates do?
>
> Do they seem to be able to sit still and concentrate longer than you can?

DO THIS: Talk to your teacher, a family member, or the school nurse about getting a checkup. Doctors and other special professionals can probably correct problems with vision, hearing, speech, and many learning difficulties so school won't be such a burden anymore.

If the English language is hard for you, ask a teacher or counselor for help. He or she can probably find a tutor or special class for you, so that you can become comfortable speaking and understanding this difficult language. Try getting involved with English-speaking activities after school. Also, ask at your local library for books or tapes designed to help people improve their speech.

And once you have connected with a speech therapist, an English-language teacher, or any other specialist—practice! Remember, the more you speak, the easier it gets!

What if
you get called on?

The thought of having to answer a teacher's question alarms some students so much that they would rather stay away from school than risk being put on the spot. Getting called on, they say, is even harder than raising their hand to volunteer to speak.

Well, it doesn't have to be so scary, as this section shows.

What if
you're afraid you won't say the *right* answer?

This is really *two What if* fears: saying the *right* answer, and *saying* the answer. Let's focus on the "right" answer in this secton and on "saying" it in the next.

Sometimes, people want so much to be right all the time, to be perfect, that they don't do anything. Do you keep quiet because you want to be sure you'll always sound good when you do open your mouth?

On page 4, you discovered how important it is to participate in some way, even if you don't always have the right answer. This really makes sense when you remember that you are in school to learn. If you already knew everything, you wouldn't need to be there at all!

But even though nobody's perfect, nobody wants to make silly-sounding mistakes, either. So . . .

Try this:

THINK ABOUT this: Does it seem to you that the people who do speak always sound good? Well, listen again. You'll probably find that they do goof up sometimes (everybody does). So you might begin by getting used to the idea that you don't always have to be right.

DO THIS: Listen even harder and find out how other people handle goofs. Some may get hysterical or go silent in shame. But the more successful ones probably

say something like "Oh, that's right! I'm sorry, I forgot!"

laugh at themselves (look at page 11 again)

ask a question, or stall, or give a nonanswer (you'll find more about these techniques on page 31)

make a note in their notebooks as a way of showing the teacher their good intentions

don't make a big deal out of it.

You can try some of the things they do, and even when you're not right, you won't be wrong, either.

What if
you're afraid you can't *say* the answer?

Some people are almost always right when they answer the teacher's questions in their minds, but when they're called on, they can't seem to say that right answer out loud.

   If that sounds like you, all you need is practice. In case you don't believe that . . .

Try this:

THINK ABOUT the fact that you are usually able to answer those questions in your mind. That probably means that it's being put on the spot that makes you nervous.

So think about ways to avoid being put on the spot. Since it's usually easier to speak when you choose to than when you're called on, why not volunteer?

DO THIS: Begin by raising your hand to ask questions, because it's harder to "make a mistake" when you ask a question. Go through your homework assignments and make a list of questions to ask. Practice asking them beforehand. Then ask!

You can practice answering questions, too. All of your homework involves questions: questions the teacher has told you to answer on paper or questions at the back of a chapter you're supposed to read. (Even math involves questions: Each problem asks "How much?") So when you do your homework, don't just write down the answers. Ask them to yourself out loud, and answer them out loud. (For an even better exercise, have someone ask you the questions, fast and out of order, just like in class.) Then, when the teacher asks those questions, you have practiced saying the answers, and it will be easier.

Also, read those study and review sections in your books—even if they aren't assigned!—and say the answers out loud.

And do this, too: *Imagine,* right now and before each class, that you're called on and that you answer correctly. Then, when you are called on during the next class discussion, you will probably be able to respond almost easily.

Is putting in this extra work for a while worth it to develop your speaking-up skills? Sure it is.

What if
you're afraid you won't *know* the answer?

Maybe you have trouble figuring out and remembering the answers. Well, in case you think that knowing the answers means knowing *all* the answers *all* the time, look at pages 26–27 about being a perfectionist, and calm down.

But it may be that the work assigned in a subject is really too hard. If so, talk to your teacher about getting extra help. Also, find some classmates who are good in the subject and do homework with them. (You *do* do the homework, don't you? If not, why not? That could solve all of your speaking-up problems.)

But if just doing homework doesn't make you "smart" enough to answer questions in class, you may need a special kind of "smarts." So . . .

Try this:

THINK ABOUT why you don't know the answers. If it is because you have trouble remembering what you've learned, you can lock the information in your head.

DO THIS:

Try studying smarter. After you've done your homework in each subject, review all your answers. This will help to keep them in your mind— and so will saying them out loud.

Review the answers again in the morning, before you go to school.

Right before each class, go over them again, to refresh your memory of them.

During class, answer in your mind every question the teacher asks, even when you don't get called on.

You might also want to review the tips on page 29.

But what if the teacher picks you to answer, say, question *A,* and you're not sure about *A* but you do know about *B.* Then

say: "I'm not exactly sure about *A,* but I do know about *B,*" or "Is that the same idea as in *B,* where it's . . . ?" or

stall: "Could you repeat the question, please?" or repeat the teacher's question yourself and in the time you've bought, glance at your notes or book. (Unless the teacher tells you otherwise, always keep your homework or book for that subject open in front of you. It's not cheating to look!)

Being smart about facts is only part of school success; *using* "smarts" is important, too.

What if
you think you're stupid?

Okay, now we're getting down to it. Since it's the fast ones, the loud ones, who make the biggest impression, people tend to think that the ones who are quiet, who are more cautious, aren't as bright. It stands to reason, then, that you might think that about yourself. (Remember pages 4 and 5 and your impression of other people in your class.)

Remember, too, that teachers may tend to ignore the quiet students—and if they're very busy, they might even assume that silence means "stupidity."

So it's no wonder that you might worry about this yourself. If you do, then . . .

Try this:

THINK ABOUT this: You're *not* stupid. Get that straight. After all, you're reading this book, aren't you? You're thinking hard about some of the new ideas you find here. "Stupid" would be not being aware of having a problem. Even more stupid would be being aware of it but not trying to do something about it.

DO THIS: Recall your record since you began school. How have your grades been? Your test scores? Your marks on projects that don't involve speaking up?

They're probably not so bad, are they? If they could be better, think again: Practically everything you do in school involves language. If you have trouble with language, look at pages 22–23. Problems with English or hearing or speech don't mean stupidity, either.

Now, make a list of all the things you are good at—all the things you've done that you are proud of. Look at the list. You'll probably see something like this.

You may be better at art or at things you do with your hands than at schoolwork.

You may be better at writing than at talking, at math than at English.

Remember that not everyone is "smart" about the same things. So instead of focusing on what you're "dumb" at, list in your mind, over and over, all the things you're smart at.

Remember, too, that not every school subject is easy for everyone. The way to get "smart" at anything—and to get some good attention and practice at speaking up, too—is to ask questions. The only stupid questions are the ones that don't get asked.

What if
you have to make a report?

You may never raise your hand to speak. You may always be able to dodge being called on. But there are some times when you must speak in class whether you want to or not. Most kids—and grown-ups, too—will tell you (when they're being honest) that everything that makes them nervous about *any* speaking-up situation comes together and gets worse when they have to speak in front of a group of people.

But every now and then, every student has to stand up in front of the room and give some kind of talk or make some kind of report. This section will help you to get past the "Oh, no" you may feel like shouting when your teacher tells you that you have to make an oral report.

What if
you're afraid to make a report?

This is another *What if* that really has two parts: being afraid, and making a report. Let's look at "being afraid" here.

Speaking up, especially while *standing* before a group, frightens some people so much that they feel literally sick. Do you ever . . . feel sick to your stomach, sweat a lot, get red in the face, feel your heart beat fast and loud, get dizzy, feel like you can't breathe, shake?

Those feelings can be scary. You may even think that you *are* sick, or that you're going to die. But those feelings are really just some of your body's normal reactions to fear or danger. Faced with a threat, your body, like that of any other animal, gets ready to fight it off by pumping out extra energy, oxygen, and blood. When there's nothing real to fight, all of those extras churn around and make you feel awful.

It's not likely that you face real physical dangers in class. But you may think having to speak up in class *is* "threatening," so your body reacts as though you were in danger. Plus, you may have what feels like a battle going on inside you: Your body wants to do one thing, and your mind another. You know you want to speak up, but you want to run away, too. That conflict can cause an anxiety attack that *feels* like terror.

Now it's fine to understand that your physical reactions are "normal," but they are still awful. So what can you do?

Try this:

THINK ABOUT and ACCEPT the fact that your body reacts to the fear it feels, even if your mind won't admit you're afraid. Next, go back to the list of *What if*'s in the table of contents and read the pages for the classroom situations that seem most often to cause such fear reactions. For instance, if you need practice in saying words out loud, see page 29; if you're worried about how to deal with the kinds of attention you'll get, see pages 11 and 13. These examples will remind you that those situations are not really threats—and will give you actions to handle your body's *reactions.*

DO THIS: Practicing some exercises will also help make the feelings go away. When you face a scary speaking-up situation . . .

breathe deeply. With your mouth closed, use your nose to pull a big breath *slowly* from the bottom of your lungs. Count to four while you do it. Hold that breath for four more counts and open your mouth to let the breath out slowly. Do this four times and feel yourself relax.

tense and loosen your muscles. Starting with your hands and feet, tighten every muscle in your body. Hold that for four counts and then slowly relax every muscle, ending with your fingers and toes. Do this four times, too.

imagine yourself calm. Close your eyes and picture yourself speaking clearly. Feel yourself speaking without fear. Run that "tape" over and over in your mind. Or imagine that you're not there in class, having to talk, but doing or seeing something that you really love, that makes you feel calm and happy. Pretend that you're "there" when you get ready to speak up.

Although humans have bodies that react like other animals' to fear, we have minds that can control and redirect that fear. So before you decide these exercises are too silly to work, try them!

Feeling confident about the *content* of a report will also help make you less afraid. But . . .

What if
you don't know how to make a report?

There are two basic stages in making any kind of report—preparation and presentation. If you've *prepared* for it well, you'll have an easier time with the part that may be scary—*presenting* it. So before you start worrying about the presentation, focus on the preparation.

> Go over the assignment as soon as you get it, and if you have any questions about it or about the topic, check with the teacher right away!

> Schedule yourself (make notes on a calendar) so that you'll have the report's contents ready well in time to allow for practice. Even if you have a lot of time, start gathering whatever you'll need now. Jot down ideas for what you want to say.

> Follow the instructions: If you're supposed to turn in an outline ahead of time, for instance, do it. May you (must you) use charts, pictures, or other visuals in your presentation? Are you supposed to read your report? Talk from notes? Speak without notes? Turn in a written version of the report? Find out ahead of time!

In preparing your report, it's helpful to write out something whether you have to turn it in or not. In simple outline, a talk (1) says what you're *going* to tell, (2) *tells* it, and (3) summarizes what you've *told.* You fill in the blanks in that outline from the research or reading you've done according to what the teacher has assigned.

The goal of preparation? To make presentation almost easy, so . . .

Try this:

THINK ABOUT your goals for the presentation of your report:

A. to get a good grade
B. to keep your audience, classmates, and teacher interested
C. to get through it with as little fear as possible.

To achieve those goals, DO THIS:

A. Since good preparation goes a long way toward getting that good grade, follow the tips on the previous page.
B. Your audience will stay interested if you keep your report short and to the point; use as many visual aids and other distractions as you can (charts, pictures, or maps; and how about real examples—plants, artwork, rocks, animals—related to your topic?); and possibly even use some of the special talents you've listed from page 15 to give your talk some zing.
C. The tips in *A* and *B* will help you to achieve goal *C* and get through it. But you'll probably feel nervous anyway (everybody does). So *practice!* Prepare far enough in advance so that you have lots of time to practice. Say your talk out loud to yourself while looking in a mirror. Tape it and play it back. Then say it in front of a friend or family member, and listen to his or her ideas for making it better. Practice *relaxing,* too: Follow all the suggestions you'll find on page 37. Keep doing them until right before you have to start talking.

And when you do get up to speak, the best thing to say first is, "I'm kind of nervous." You'll be amazed at how much easier your report is after you admit that! Then take a deep breath, and go to it. You *can* speak up.

What if
you hate being stared at?

"All that is fine," you may say. "I can prepare, and practice, and take a deep breath—but then I get up, and everybody is *staring* at me, and I just hate it!"

For many people, it's that feeling of being the center of attention that makes them feel sick or weak in the knees. You may not even be able to make words come out of your mouth when people are looking at you.

If you have such a strong reaction to speaking before a group of people, you probably won't ever really like it. But there are some ways to make it possible, so . . .

Try this:

THINK ABOUT the ideas on page 13, and try those tips. It's especially important for you to practice your talk as much as possible in front of real people—your family or friends. Not only will this get you accustomed to speaking before a group, but the better you know your talk, the more you can concentrate just on keeping calm. (You might also want to think about volunteering to talk in front of small groups like one of your clubs or your scout troop—any group that doesn't make you feel nervous. That way, you can get practice in a safe setting.) You should also put extra effort into the fear-reducing exercises on page 37.

When you stand up to speak, DO THIS: Pick one person (preferably near the back of the room) to talk to. That way, you won't really be speaking to a crowd but just telling another individual what you have to say. Let a friend know you're going to talk "to" him or her. Or just pick a spot on the back wall of the room and look at that while you talk. Let the rest of the room and the people in it disappear.

If you can hold papers, note cards, charts, or illustrations without shaking, fine—that gives you something to do with your hands. If not, put any notes you need on a desk and clasp your hands behind you as much as possible. Then take a deep breath and let the first words out of your mouth be something like "Boy, am I nervous!" or "I hate this, but I'm going to try it anyway." Let yourself laugh, and listen to others laugh with you—lots of people know how you feel!

What if
you *still* can't speak up?

Nobody said that speaking up was easy: In fact, this book agrees with you that it's hard. But what if you've thought hard about all the questions in the book so far and seriously practiced all the tips, and you still can't speak up?

You don't have to give up. This section will give you some more tips on speaking up.

What if
you're "only" shy?

Being shy is not a problem that many people seem to pay much attention to—probably for the same reason that a teacher pays less attention to the student who is quiet. Shyness just doesn't seem as important to anyone—teachers, parents, people in general—as the kinds of obvious defects that cause trouble, not just for the troubled, but for others as well.

But shyness *is* a problem—if you're shy, you know that! The fact that others don't take it seriously only makes it worse, and that may make you feel like nobody else is shy.

Lots of people are shy, but they can't talk about it easily because—well, because they're shy. Plus, people make jokes about shyness. Some even think it's "cute."

What can you do? Well . . .

Try this:

If you're aware that you're shy, an important first step is to accept it in yourself. Being shy *isn't* "bad" or "stupid," but shyness can create extra hurdles for you, in class and out, so . . .

THINK ABOUT what it means to be shy and about what you might do to overcome it. "Shy" may be another word for afraid. But a lot of the pages in this book have talked about overcoming fear, so try what they suggest. Shy may also mean cautious—it only makes sense to stand back a bit and observe a situation before plunging in. Be gentle with yourself, but take a look at the look-around-you tips on pages 9, 11, and 19, and try imitating some more outgoing behavior. If you're *too* shy, you won't be able to enjoy the pleasure that other people can bring to your life.

DO THIS:

Imagine yourself feeling *comfortable* joining in conversations and activities. (See page 37 for help in imagining.)

Find other people who seem shy and make friends with them. Being with them (or just observing them) can help you handle the more outspoken people who make you feel really shy.

Try those suggestions for dealing with being laughed at (page 11)— especially the hint about laughing at yourself. Learning to laugh at your shyness in a nice way can make it go away.

And each day, try to talk to at least one person you don't have to talk to. The more you do it, the easier it gets. Soon, it will be easy in class, too.

What if you're just naturally nervous?

Each person's nervous system is different. You may indeed be higher-strung than other people. Do you seem more physically bothered by worries, loud noises, scary stories than other kids you know? Do you have a hard time sitting still? Are you a light sleeper? Do you often find your hands or jaws clenched? Do you bite your nails or play with your fingers a lot? Chances are, you've always been like that, since you were a baby (ask your parents). Some people seem literally to have more sensitive nerves, more muscle tension than others, so they get more nervous and tense when they have to speak. You can adapt, though. So . . .

Try this:

DO THIS: If you're a naturally nervous person, you'd do well to put some extra effort into those relaxing exercises on page 37.

Get some extra physical exercise, too: Even if you don't care for sports or games, make a habit of walking or working out. This kind of physical activity can "work out" a lot of your natural tensions. And it's especially useful right before you're supposed to give a talk.

Check your diet. Do you eat mostly well-balanced meals of "real" food—or a lot of fast-food snacks? Stick to the basics and stay away from sweets and cola drinks or anything else that contains caffeine; a body like yours doesn't need that kind of lift.

And don't expect to get mellow. Instead, get to know your own special reactions and patterns; accept them and work with them. "Naturally nervous" means you also have a lot of energy. Instead of trying to fight it, let some of that energy come out when you need to speak up in class.

What if
you *still* don't like to speak up?

Will it *ever* be easy? Even though

> you know why it's important to speak in class
>
> you have a pretty good idea of why it's hard for you
>
> you believe that lots of other people have the same trouble as you do with speaking in class
>
> you know you're not stupid
>
> you've learned how to prepare for class so that you know enough right answers, and you know what to say when you aren't sure of an answer
>
> you've tried to practice some of the tips that this book has suggested so far . . .

you find that you *still* don't like to speak in class!

That's okay. But remember this: Many people manage to do many things that they don't like to do. They talk themselves into it (or even trick themselves into it), and then they just *do* it.

You can, too, if you . . .

Try this:

THINK ABOUT and ACCEPT the fact that you don't like speaking up. It's just a part of you. You can even tell yourself out loud, "I hate this! I hate it, and it scares me—but I'm going to do it anyway." If you can, tell somebody else how much you hate it, too. Talking about it honestly takes away some of its power, and you'll begin to feel better.

DO THIS: You don't really have to like to speak in class, but you can "act as if" you do. Pretend that you are good at it and that it's fun. Pretend that you aren't going to be speaking in class but just talking to a friend. Before school, imagine that it's all over with—and imagine how good you'll feel then, especially when you've made yourself talk in class that day.

When you do speak in class, tell yourself that you're still practicing. The more often you can force yourself into speaking by fooling yourself into it, the more you will speak, and the better at it you will get—even if you may never really like it.

In the meantime, remember that there are lots of ways to make up for the speaking up you're not quite ready to do:

spend extra time and energy on other school projects

do your homework with extra care

study extra hard for tests and quizzes

think up extra-credit projects that don't involve talking.

It may even be that if you stop worrying so much about speaking up and start concentrating instead on making your mark in other ways, you'll be surprised to find that, without even thinking about it, you are speaking up in class.

What if
you just want to give up?

Okay, so you've followed all the suggestions in this book, raised your hand, opened your mouth . . . and it was still hard to get the words out easily. Now you're thinking that it's hopeless and you will never be able to do it, so why bother trying again?

Well, before you give up entirely, remind yourself of the benefits to be gained from speaking up—the obvious ones and the hidden ones. This book lists some obvious ones on page 5, but you'll probably have some of your own reasons to add to it.

Now, decide which is the most important benefit for *you*. Set that as a goal and think about it every time you feel like not speaking up.

Think about this, too: By learning to speak up in class, you gain some extra benefits, as well. For instance . . .

you may find it easier to speak up outside of class

you'll probably find some new friends

you'll feel more confident in other social situations

by feeling better about yourself, you'll probably be able to try a lot of other new things that once made you nervous

you'll learn the steps to take to solve *any* tough personal problem.

Aren't these benefits good enough to give speaking up in class another try? If you think so, then . . .

Try this:

THINK ABOUT it: Whether you want to shoot more baskets, learn a new dance, or learn to play the saxophone or the piano, you need practice. Speaking up comfortably in class takes practice, too.

DO THIS:

Find a place where it's private. Then practice raising your hand. Do it again and again in private; then you will be used to doing it in public.

Practice saying the answers to questions—the ones in your textbooks, and even those on TV game shows.

Practice saying a whole series of words out loud. Begin in private by reading out loud in front of a mirror, maybe with only your pet in the room. Then, instead of reading out loud, say something else, like your name and your age, for instance, and something about yourself.

Make a point of talking when you're with your family or with a good friend. Talking about anything at all will give your speaking-up skills the exercise they need.

And remember—the more you can talk about your worries about raising your hand, being called on, making a report . . . the sooner you will find that you *can* speak up in class.

What if you want to find out more about speaking?

You may have found in this book a topic you'd like to know more about. Or you may have focused on a speaking-up problem that you would like more help with. If so, try reading some more about the subject.

Try this:

Look in the library. You'll find books that explain the physical act of speech, like *Wonders of Speech* by Alvin and Virginia Silverstein (Morrow Junior Books, 1988) or *Speech and Language Disorders* by Gilda Berger (Franklin Watts, 1981), and books that discuss *public* speaking, like *So You Have to Give a Speech* by Margaret Ryan (Franklin Watts, 1987) or *You Mean I Have to Stand Up & Say Something?* by Joan Detz (Macmillan, 1986).

Also ask your librarian for other suggestions and for help in finding articles in magazines and in encyclopedias.

If you want to find help or information on special needs, write or phone these organizations to find out where to get it.

The American Speech, Language, and Hearing Association
10801 Rockville Pike
Rockville, MD 20852
(301) 897-5700

The Speech Communications Association
5105 Backlick Road
Annandale, VA 22003
(703) 750-7033

The more you find out, the more you will realize that you *can* speak up in class.

Index